NO SUCH THING AS HALFWAY

~ɩ𝒹ℓ~

ACHU 'RIFLEX' EBONG MBA

Stuck in The Middle
&
UpsideDown Movement

PRAISE FOR ACHU EBONG MBA'S
NO SUCH THING AS HALFWAY

"Achu Ebong Mba's debut novel is a heart wrenching tale of the audacity of love and its daring to bend the callous hands of Tribalism towards its destiny. This beautifully crafted story juxtaposes the conflicts and confines of ethnic purity against the influence of desire and fate."

Jason Makwein Nkwain, Creator and Curator of The Of One Blood Project.

*

"Gripping, heartbreaking, and ultimately timely. This is a spectacular debut novel."

Manekeu N Ndoping. Published blogger, avid book reader.

*

"In a beautiful yet searing drama, Achu's amazing narrative leaps off the page with its urgency and power. It's almost impossible not to empathize with their grief, may it be felt deeply."

Rogerick Brown

*

"Brilliant! Achu Ebong Mba is an amazing storyteller.

This is a necessary read."

Fotemah Mba, J.U.M.P Africa Founder, Books for Africa Board Member

*

"Not every story or chapter in life fits nicely and not every prayer for things "to go smoothly" actually gets answered. Life is sometimes very complicated, and some stories are exquisitely painful. When I think of how the Bible speaks of suffering, I now have a different category of suffering that I must now include after reading this intense book. It's the suffering of a romantic tragedy caused by the clash of family cultures. Their story is as C.S. Lewis would say is "A Severe Mercy". (This book actually reminds me of that book). The severity of the pain that insists on being attended to has drawn them closer to the perfect maker, redeemer, and lover of their souls. There is a particular like in the book where Yonas considers himself a "damn fool". Well, in the eternal story of scripture, God's son loved us so much that he became a "Damn fool" on the cross so that we might come to see that the foolishness of God's wiser than men. God is no fool in his love for us and no character in this story is either. May the reader see for themselves. Take up and read.

Charlie Baile, Senior Pastor Shady Grove Presbyterian Church

ISBN: 978-1-7347982-0-3

First Edition

Cover Art: Akil Alleyne
Editor: Lesley-Anne Longo
Advisor: Akondi N Mba
Illustration: Vanessa Mendozzi
Interior Design: Lorna Reid

First Printing 2020

Printed in the United States of America

IAMRIFLEX.COM

A Novel by

ACHU 'RIFLEX' EBONG MBA

*

Inspired by real events.

For the next generation.

For Asher and Liam.

For those who have been through it or are going through it.

And, as always, for my son.

ACKNOWLEDGEMENTS

I would like to express my gratitude to a few individuals who were very instrumental in the creation of this book. First, Jason, an author, filmmaker, teacher, and a great friend. You inspired me with your grind over the years to bring your many projects to life and it was my absolute honor to share with you the very first draft of this novel at its rawest form. Being the very first person to read it at that stage of its creation, you gave me the encouragement, criticism, and honest judgement that I didn't even know I needed, and that would push me to work harder. I'm very much looking forward to the impact your project, Of One Blood, has on our society and it's always a delight speaking with you brother. Keep grinding.

Secondly, I want to thank my brother Akondi. Growing up you were brilliant in Mathematics and I wasn't, I chose arts and language because I just wasn't good with numbers but and I'm grateful your supported me in my arts. You've hooked me up over the years with awesome things like the spectacular web site we have and even though you get on my last nerves, I love you man. I've got horror stories to tell me kids of our growing up and I'm certain you'll make a dope uncle. Throughout my creative process of writing you would always press me to read the book at its premature stages, citing its your right as my brother, and I'm sorry to have made you wait like everybody else. I hope it's worth it.

Kelyne, I appreciate you a lot and thank you for being long suffering, for your prayers, sacrifices, and indulgence throughout this process.

I also would like to thank Afia. You are strong, you are unbelievably brave, and a blessing to the world.

Finally, thank you to Masazew Mba, Tatiana Nchotu, Relindis Mbah, Adel Kamara, Simon Asare, and Will Anyu who all made generous monthly membership subscriptions to my Patreon, which was extremely useful in bringing this dream of mine to life. You guys are the best Patrons.

I also would like to dedicate this book to my son.

FOREWORD

꧁꧂

By Temidayo Akinsanya
President, Truth & Culture Incorporated

To choose between people you have known for your entire life and someone you have known for only a couple of years is a fairly easy choice to make. But what if this person you have known for only a couple of years has captured your heart? What if this person has walked with you on a journey toward love and self-discovery in a way no other soul has? What if this individual is the one your soul desires for the rest of your breathing days? Then, the decision no longer seems like a fairly easy choice to make. It becomes complicated and difficult.

This is the journey that my friend Achu 'RifleX' Ebong Mba will take you on in this sobering book. It is a journey that speaks to anyone who has experienced making hard decisions that did not merely lack the approval of treasured family members, but even more, those family members worked intently to sabotage the decision. It is not only for those with a first-person understanding of such experiences, but there is also extra room on the journey for the curious eyes who wonder what such an experience would feel like.

This much is clear: Having to make decisions under such circumstances carries a heavy cost that one must be aware of and be willing to pay. The cost of now having disgruntled and dis-affectionate family members, the cost of being displaced by the same family members, or perhaps even worse, the cost of a broken heart when one abandons the romantic relationship.

Turn the page and enter into the adventure of life. An adventure that is sure to leave you asking questions that do not have satisfactory answers. But isn't that how life works? We engage on a day-to-day basis, seeking answers to life's challenging questions, but with no one to provide that which eliminates the pain and the mystery behind the questions.

This is not a book about finding answers to the questions of life, but of experiencing the dilemmas that arise in life and witnessing the resolutions that are attempted. .

PREFACE

I learned how to walk and read at the same time in the third grade and have never looked up since. My second-oldest sister kept boxes upon boxes of books, particularly romance novels, in the family home where I grew up, so I spent my formative years hiding away in my room and reading novels I had no business reading at that stage in my life. These days, my bookcases are stacked with theological books, Bible commentaries, biographies, memoirs, and pamphlets.

In high school, I was among the very first to raise a hand to volunteer for passage readings in the classroom. I took on English as my major when I went to college, partially to escape the Mathematics subjects and boring sciences, but mainly to hone and polish my skills for critical reading and thinking public speaking, and creative writing. The teachers and professors I had the privilege of learning from throughout my educational years have all had a hand in making me the lover of written pieces that I am today. I do hope this book somehow lands in any one of their hands and they read it with pride.

I remember when I moved to the United States of America at the age of fourteen years old with my family, I was placed in the English As A Second or Foreign Language (ESOL) class. At first, I felt somewhat insulted, as I thought my English was just fine. However, it only took two days for the teacher to realize I didn't belong there, and my English was just as excellent as the kid in Advanced Placement (AP) English. But that's the same energy I have gotten pretty much my entire adult life whenever I meet certain people.

"Your English sounds amazing for an immigrant, Achu!" some would say. Or, "You learned how to speak English when you moved here, didn't you? Or do you guys speak English in your country?" some would ask. While the latter remarks may sound more like an ignoramus making a genuine inquisition, I never take offense to any of it and have come to use these remarks as fuel to challenge myself more in the field of literature by making a timeless contribution.

It's a blessing to have been raised in the West African culture and also a tremendous benefit that my family strives to keep our culture, language, and even food traditions steeped into our everyday life. It's a running joke among people of the African community living in my metropolitan area that, if you get a visa to come to the United States and decide to settle Maryland, then you really haven't left Africa. In essence, you just moved the better neighborhood. The reason behind this joke is the immense population of Africans from all corners of the continent and fellow countrymen you will find yourself rubbing shoulders with. The lounges and clubs are packed with them, and the DJs play our music exclusively. The food is readily available in the countless international supermarkets, and in any aunt's house, you visit. The language and shared jokes are understood. In short, everything is the same. It's something we cherish and hold dearly.

On the other side of this beauty is the negative aspect, which is why this book had to be written, the purpose of this book. With our great pride in preserving our culture comes a practice of clinging to the traditional ways of doing things, the customs our parents have held on to for decades, maybe even centuries. The elders have crossed over the pond, but have refused to open their minds to the world around them, to new and brighter ideas, cultures, or people. As a result of this, the vast majority of us who are first-generation children are limited in a lot of the choices we are offered. Even in education—which is mandatory-you only get a handful, either a lawyer, a doctor, or an engineer is what you are expected to become. "I didn't fly you halfway across the world to come and disgrace me, to come and bring shame to this family!" our parents would warn as they pushed you into a school that probably wasn't your school of choice. "So-and-so down the street's daughter went to such-and-such school and is now a lawyer!" a mother would say in comparison to her daughter.

It's all for bragging rights in the community, especially who your son weds or what family your daughter marries into. Parents seldom consider the long-term happiness and mental well-being of their child, and that has led to increased rates of children lying to their parents about what it is they are actually studying in school, or students graduating from many years of university and 'medical school only to find the field detestable after only a few months in the real world, leading to a search for a new career. Worst of all, this has led to increasing numbers of unhappy marriages or even divorces. Beyond the walls of safety that one's culture provides is what the profound embryonic imagination tells us is a monster. We become xenophobic for pragmatic reasons, whether or not we manifest it in overt racism. We would love to think we live in a landscape of diversity and equality on how we view and treat our neighbors, but any freedom we have is dependent on barriers to keep the monster out.

I have heard and read stories of hundreds of young men and women here in the diaspora and back home in the continent who have been literally forced into relationships and marriages, by their families, against their wishes, and personally know a handful of people who have suffered the misfortune of set arrangements not ending well in the long run, though much to the joy of the couples involved and the organizers some live happily and long enough to enjoy its fruits. I equally know of and have heard the stories of the few who dared to resist and fight for freedom of choice and for their love.

To be clear, this is definitely not a blanket reality. It should not be taken to mean this is the dynamic in every household, or for every kid or with every immigrant parent. There is some beauty in arranging a marriage or connection between two people. Many of our parents are the result of this practice and it works for the majority of them. My mother, for example, was told at 19 years old her husband was my dad a 33-year-old military man making his way up the ranks, while she'd never set eyes on him or knew of his existence. Thirty-five plus years into their marriage now with six children, they enjoy the fruit of family, love, and patience. There are the cool ones, the ones who are living in 2035, while the rest are in the 1970s stuck in the opposite side of tribalism. The latter are those who inspired this book, along with the plight of the many young men and women who have been stripped of the love of their life by authorities such as the family, or who had to let go of that authority, the family, in order to cleave on to a new future with the person they love and wish to build a new reality with. And my own family isn't exempt from it as I have experienced it first-hand.

I one hundred percent believe I have more than enough qualifications to address this very delicate subject in this book as to some degree I have passed through this plight myself. The heart-wrenching consequence of our closed-minded beloved brothers and sisters, parents, and relatives both in the continent and the diaspora with antiquated views is why this book exists. This book is the result of over five years of blood, sweat and tears spent I have spent and cried with friends, relatives, and internet stories who have suffered to make a relationship work.

The following story may be considered a memoir, and the reality rings true for thousands of men and women, not only in the African community but across the globe who will find themselves in these characters. It reflects the author's present recollection of experiences over time. Some names and characteristics have been changed, some events have been compressed, and some dialogue has been recreated. My aim is to add a credible voice to a conversation that, for years, has been under wraps. My goal is to start or reignite a dialogue about solutions. I don't claim to know the answer to every unique situation, but I do know that with everything in life comes communication, healing, and understanding as a community and people. May this book spark that conversation and bring forth a healthy harmony between our people.

I hope you see our beloved friends Yonas and Demi as just a figment of a resounding many across the world. This is a story of the strength and beauty of love—the power and beauty of family. And the forte and attractiveness of growth. As you read ask yourself the question, I have asked many who engaged in these conversations with me. How can we, and how should we love the stranger? True love is an act. A doing. And by this, I mean relationships, not a feeling or an attitude. We must form a relationship in order to best love a person. Pretending to love that person simply because they are other, or a stranger just doesn't cut it.

On the other hand, that creates a gap between us, and an unreal image of that person, which in the end takes us much further away from their mysterious and attractive strangeness. Read with care. Read with empathy. Thank you for picking it up

CHAPTER ONE

SLIDE IN THE DMS

Tayo's dreadlocks quivered as he shook his head in utter disbelief, sinking into the leather couch as he clenched his hands in frustration with what he had just heard.

"Yonas," he said in shock, staring into my brown eyes burning with anger and sadness, "Are you, serious man!? What century are we living in?" he added with a roar. Tayo, a young man from Liberia, newly wedded to a young lady from Benin, had been my close confidant for over a year now. He absorbed the painful story I had just shared, maintaining the kindness that I knew I could always expect from him. Despite his frustration on my behalf, his concern for me shone through.

"I kid you not, man," I responded with a halfhearted shrug. "This is, without a doubt, the hardest thing I have had to endure. I wouldn't wish this on my worst enemy!" I added. My eyes shifted laterally and became glazed with a glossy layer of tears. I tried not to blink fearing they would pour from her eyelids, drenching my cheeks.

If I had a dollar for every time anybody who knew me, was familiar with my situation and was rooting for me asked for an update on my sad state of affairs, I'd probably be rich. But I had always given surface answers to people. Even my very good friend, O.G., who I shared everything with, was only allowed to hear the whole story once it got too unbearable to discuss, for it was like tearing open a scar every time I had to explain. My mentor, spiritual leaders, and a few confidants were the only people who knew the whole story, who knew of my plight.

It was different at this moment with Tayo, not only because he was learning of the sad state of the matter as it stood for me, but because I knew he genuinely cared and would listen with a sympathetic heart. He himself had gone down the same path that I was now traveling, so I felt comfortable opening up to him. As I spoke, the tears I had held back for so many months came bursting forth like water from a broken dam. Everything at the moment was raw. Fresh tears, and raw emotions, as I poured out my frustration and hurt to Tayo, who listened so attentively.

"I'm telling you, bro, if I were a character, and my

life was a tragedy, you can bet that my fatal flaw would be my desire to be understood," I said.

I hadn't even gotten a quarter into my story yet when Tayo whispered to me, "Bro, you definitely need to write a book about this. A lot of our people can relate. You of all people know I am among that number," echoing what I had heard from others who knew what I was going through or who I had consulted for advice or prayer. Having gone through it himself and experienced the affliction of it, he knew it would be an inspiration and encouragement to the many we knew in the same predicament.

My heart had been freshly broken, and I was filled with anger. Upset, frustrated, and in pain, I could only borrow the words of a hood philosopher from Fort Myers, Florida named Algernod Washington, "I'm big mad!"

*****

At this point in my life, I wasn't checking for a girl. Fresh out of a very toxic relationship and just newly born again, as in a new believer in Christ, I was focused, locked in, my mind fixed on just a handful of things, and adding a relationship to the list was definitely not a priority. To me, love was a huge distraction, and if I wasn't at campus Bible study, I was either in my dorm room working on one of the many homework assignments I had due every other week, or composing and recording music in my makeshift dorm room recording studio. Nine times out of ten, I was most likely making music. That was pretty much all I cared about at the time, and all I wanted to do—just create.

On campus, I was one of the very few people who had a studio set up in their dorm room. In a historically black university, everybody, their friend, and their friend's friend is a rapper in our community. If you aren't rapping, you are trapping, and in college, there aren't any real trappers, so we're all rappers or scholars.

This is how I came to collaborate on a very dope track with a homie and good friend who went by the stage name of Jin Rari. Jin Rari was a thorough spitter, very talented, and one of the few who took the music thing nearly as seriously as I did. It wasn't a hobby or just a fun thing to do but a legitimate source of income and medium for creativity. We collaborated on a song called "Every Time," which we co-produced and wrote together as young guys who just enjoyed the art or rap and wanted to create good music to be consumed in great scale. Jin Rari had spent some time in Houston, Texas for a church event some months back, and always bragged to us about how solid the believers out there were. Especially the sisters. He was Nigerian, and while there, he got to spend ample time with the vast Nigerian community in Houston.

Being the college boys that we were, and young single Christian men, most of whom were very interested in dating and marriage, his descriptions of these sisters down South made the brothers want to hop on the next flight out on a one-way ticket with no intentions of returning. It was like the discovering of a new galaxy far away yet so near that it had to be beholden. Genuine men and women of God and fine sisters. Prayed-up, Christ-exalting sisters. Very well cultured and yet westernized sisters, now that's a rare balance to come across. During our recording sessions, Jin Rari spoke of these sisters for days, in a manner that would almost make you pity him for having to return. But we were young men still growing in life and education and hopeless with just these thoughts. It didn't hurt to imagine as it wasn't practically attainable. But of course, we did ask and inquire a lot, frequently, just praying and trusting that maybe one day, the good Lord would allow our paths to cross somehow.

Lo and behold, when "Every Time" was released, a couple of those same Texas brothers and sisters who had been following Jin Rari on social media were also exposed to me. A good thing I supposed and a blessing. Meeting people who shared in the same faith and mind as you in other parts of the world. The blessing of the internet as we have it. The song generated a little online buzz of its own and gained likes and spins thanks to Jin Rari's networking and likability, which included listeners from his recent trip down South. One of these listeners was a young lady named Demi. She was different. She loved good music and took exceptional joy and pride in promoting the style, content, and genre of music we made. "Every Time" was her jam! To be sincere, the track was dope, and we had been getting great reviews all over social media. My social media mentions, and messages had been popping, but Demi's particular reaction and feedback on the song managed to cut through all the noise and gain my attention. Maybe it was her reply to my tweet of the track link with those kind and grace-filled words, or maybe it was her profile picture. All I know is, she just hit me differently. All the thought and visions of endless possibilities, so long in the telling, crowded my mind with unbelievable swiftness.

She seemed like somebody who understood music, who respected the craft, and who took care of communicating her feedback to an artist. It only took me a couple of back-and-forths in the mentions to recognize that she was a person who loved music on another level, and who was appreciative of that particular track. I needed to know more about her. So, I slid in her DMs. The conversation didn't have to stay centered around music, but I had to carry it on. Hoping it didn't just last that afternoon or moment. A conversation deeper than words. The emoji choices and the grammatical usage of punctuations and clauses. I didn't think my ice-cold heart from a previously lousy romance, and dedication to my faith could be revived to dearness and beat differently, for anything more than friendship. Still, it jolted at Demi's warm spirit, and I felt the spark of a discerning interest. I was polite and friendly. She responded with a sweet and pleasant enthusiasm.

*****

A "ding" came from my cell phone as it vibrated on the wooden table it sat peacefully on. I immediately recognized the name of the sender ID because I had recently checked her out after a few mentions and likes, conversations, and the occasional "that's dope" or "amen."

"How can I be praying for you, bro?" the message read. It was from Demi.

I just about fell out of my seat in awe. My mind was racing at a speed of approximately 100 miles an hour, speculating on the motive behind her asking to be praying for me, and how I might respond. Surely this is just normal, right? I thought to myself. People do pray for other people. This was most definitely praiseworthy; this is that kind of thing that gets you praising the good Lord. It's not often that you get a sister hitting you up directly to ask how she can lift you up in her prayer. It's different when you're in a Bible study connect group setting, and someone shares a prayer request or something, but this? No, this was divine, this was a different level of bold, a different level of sincere. I didn't know this girl from Adam, but after this message alone, goodness, I knew I needed to know her. We needed to be friends. These are the type of people you need in your life; I thought to myself—a person who wants to pray for you without even really knowing you—a person who cared for your spirit.

"I've got a concert tomorrow that I'm currently cutting a mix for, and my main goal is not only to have a good set, but to communicate the gospel to my audience. Truth be told, it is always a terrifying thought. Standing up on that stage, performing to hundreds of people about Jesus, is a tall order. Please pray for boldness and the right words to speak, and for me to bring the truth uncompromised," I replied. Second-guessing myself if I had said too much or hadn't said enough or whatever. But I proceeded to thank her, so profoundly for her willingness to besiege God on my behalf.

Of course, I wasn't going to let this be the first and only time we spoke. I wasn't even going to follow the "two-day rule," which, in this case, would have been logical, as I would have had to report on how the concert went. No, I put my size 10 foot on the gas pedal till it hit 60mph from 0 in less 3 seconds and went for it.

I wasn't exactly sure what her motives were in asking, but one thing was for sure—she loved to talk to Jesus and about Jesus. About his kingdom, and good music. The only three things I felt equally passionately about, so we talked. A lot!

We messaged each other back and forth daily, debating weighty theological topics and concepts, chatting about events going on in each other's lives, life matters, and ministry. Weeks passed, and then months, and we were still at it in the DMs. Being the type of guy that I am and with the mindset I was in, some days, I would delay my responses, just to avoid seeming so pressed. From what I could gather and by all understanding, Demi was just herself, a kind, Jesus-loving girl who was friendly enough to chat with a "stranger" like me the way she did, with no underlying motives, just because we shared common interests and had really good conversations.

Fascinating to me the most was her love for Christian hip-hop music, and especially my music. She would let me send her lyrics I wrote, she would go through them, and we would go back and forth on whether or not I conveyed the theological concepts adequately in my rhymes. She gave very detailed and constructive criticism on what would make the music more appealing. We had a lot in common and got off to quite a riveting start.

CHAPTER TWO

ℭℓ

PULL UP

I was just a black girl minding my business, drinking my water, and reading my Bible, then this just happened. And I'm so grateful it did!" Demi would often say virtuously, with a broad smile, showing off her beautifully straight, white teeth, every time we thought back in delight over how we met. Or every time an inquiring mind asked us of the inception of our relationship.

What is behind a computer keyboard isn't always real. I have seen trolls use the internet to say what they would never say to your face, the media uses it to share breaking news and reach audiences in a faster way, and many of us use it to communicate and connect with friends, fans, and family. The pendulum swings both ways, from the twin truths that, although email, texting, and other impersonal communication mediums have developed our communication abilities, those same methods have the power to make us more cowardly, as we are able to hide behind our keyboards and mobile devices. However, while the most important issues can't always be solved through the written word, the most pivotal of moments can be created through digital words. We certainly were living in the age and took every advantage of it.

Most people will be too afraid of being catfished when talking to somebody online to ever consider taking the conversation to the next level of meeting the individual in real life. However, at this point in my life, I wasn't really checking for any girl or looking for a relationship or companionship. In my mind, I thought, we meet so many people online these days that for me, Demi was just another elegant young lady out there in the digital world whom I may or may not enjoy the pleasure of knowing from a distance. We meet new people in these spaces every day. They follow, we follow back. They unfollow. It's just the cycle.

As the months progressed, our conversation effortlessly morphed from bare name exchanges and pleasantries to daily mutual encouragement as co-laborers for the gospel of Christ in the world. And as time progressively passed, we cultivated somewhat of a routine of sharing encouraging messages, podcast sermons, and memes with each other like everyone does. Sharing the laughs and highlights of the day with the people who relate the most, all in social media, direct messaging or DMs. Eventually, we moved our chats to email where thought could be expressed at length without the constraint of character limits.

Our routine continued. I would send her samples of tracks and songs I had recorded and lyrics I had written for her opinion on the sound, quality of the rhymes, and the potential for success with my fans. To be fair, she isn't a musical genius by any stretch, knowing the ins and outs of a composition, or what arrangements would make a great record that would generate hundreds of thousands of streams, but the mere fact that she loved music and was excited to discuss it made for lots of great talks on the sound theology. I was drawn to this. We joked about me naming her my personal A&R—responsible for scouting my talent and developing me for a bigger audience. We would do this for days and weeks, emailing each other back and forth on music and chopping it over Bible passages, all while also taking the time to get to know each other on a deeper level.

The physical distance that separated us gave us no choice but to talk, and we did talk a lot. Most times, lasting well into the nights and picked right back up first thing in the mornings when we woke up. Although we shared the same continent, we were apart by many miles—I was in Baltimore, and Demi was in Houston. With a robust and ever-growing friendship and the availability of technology, it was time to introduce video chat to our arsenal of means of communication. I remember Demi being very nervous about this idea. She was overtaken with anxiousness on the day of our scheduled video chat. "All day," she would later confess to me frantically, "all day, I couldn't help myself from being tense at work. I thought about how I would act seeing you FaceTime for the first-time day long!"

I knew she was concerned about how I would perceive her looks, what girl wouldn't? For I was comfortable enough at that point to compliment her on her beauty and modesty based on what I knew and saw from social media. She was nervous at the thought of virtually meeting me for the first time, so to speak, but she wasn't sure she was ready to face this giant of a fear. We were scheduled to Video call that evening after each of us had returned from work and decompressed, sort of like a date, except it was through video call (but mentally, it felt like a date).

Demi's fear of finally meeting a guy she'd been talking to via digital texts for many months on live video was crippling, so much so that she delayed calling as arranged by almost twenty minutes. I found it extremely cute but managed to encourage her after I finally made the call myself. She panned the camera away from her face, revealing only a portion of her smooth, dark, beautiful visage, a practice she continued to do throughout the course of our relationship. It made her comfortable to talk, and I was okay with that. For once, I listened more than I spoke.

The longer we stayed on the call, the more we knew that everything—the laughs, our commonalities, and interests—was making a link between us. Demi always remained shy and nervous around me, whether virtually or physically, but that never prevented her from being articulate and holding an intellectual conversation., even with the great chasm of distance that separated us. She describes it like a swarm of butterfly in her stomach at just the sight of me or the sound of my voice—sort of like in high school, every time you see your crush.

Months passed, and our mutual interest in visiting each other grew all the more potent. Demi had been to Virginia for a young adult Christian conference but had spent most of her life in the South. Ultimately, it all worked out, as Baltimore and the nation's capital, was high up on Demi's list of cities to visit, and it only made sense to seize the opportunity to visit the nation's capital and take in everything it had to offer in a quick weekend trip. The nature of our friendship had allowed for us to grow acquainted with new mutual friends and family from each side beyond Jin Rari at this point. I had become friends with Demi's good friend and road dog, Jean. It only made sense for safety and formality. "Girl I'm riding with you! If he turns out to be crazy, I will be right there" Jean joked with a hint of gravitas.

It was the perfect scenario like divinely ordained. I was the ideal person to host and show them around the nation's capital. At this point in time, I had started catching feelings for Demi and was considering entering into a courtship relationship with her. It had been many years since my last relationship ended. My newly found and intense love for Christ kept my focus off the ladies. In fact, Demi and my good O.G. were the only people I communicated with on a deep level. I was open with Demi about my hopes for how our relationship might evolve in the future.

I'm a romantic, always have been since my formative years. It's in my nature as a Kenyan. The type to write a girl a poem or express my feelings in a handwritten letter via snail mail. One of the few guys who still believed in the process of wooing a woman, or rightly asking her to date or court. From its inception, I knew we might encounter roadblocks with this desire, her being a Nigerian and me a Kenyan, though we live in the diaspora. From my youth my family had always encouraged only dating or marrying from my tribe as was the case with her. Failure to adhere to this ultimatum has often resulted in ostracization of the children by the parents as was the case for friends and family around me. "Where there is no guidance, a people falls; but in an abundance of counselors there is safety" (Proverbs 11:14).

I was so encouraged to see Demi was taking this

warning to practice, as she demanded I give her some time to speak with her spiritual leaders about the prospect of dating me with intent to marry, and most of all, confide with her friends first. That in itself was very attractive, and all the more reason why I agreed to give her all the time she would need to get back to me with a yes or a no. I had no doubt the answer, whenever it came, would be a substantial yes because I knew our chemistry had a good spark and was growing. But to make sure of a positive response, I had to put another right foot forward. In the meantime, I had high hopes for the upcoming trip.

On the eve of the day before her trip she walked into her room, lugging her handbag and keys after a long day at the office. She was immediately greeted with the fresh scent of two dozen calla lilies and long-stemmed red roses waiting for her in a vase on her dresser. With the flowers, I had arranged for the florist to write (though not in the cleanest script) a poem:

"Dear,

When you do send me flowers,
May they come with serenading pipes of pomp and pageantry to celebrate us,
In our fullest glory of the perfecting love of our flawed humanity,
When you do send me flowers,

May they come with listening petal ears and countless comforting hugs to calm my anxiety and soothe my aches,
When you do send me flowers,
May they come with the loving understanding that sometimes it is okay that I do want to be left alone with no violation of my healing space…with a very palpable praying and present silence of your unspeakable care that recognizes, I need you close but not so close, just close enough…
When you do send me flowers,
May they never come for the first time to mourn my departure, to regret my going, to court my never to return presence for dispelling the vacuum-sucking void of my absence,

The departed abhorrently despise those who send them their first flowers in the form of mourning wreaths,
They couldn't care less for that hypocritical mess,
So, God to thee this day I pray never to be the one who sends my first flowers in the form of mourning wreaths,
When you do send me flowers,
Whether they be plucked blooming roses, orchids and the wildest lilies of countless hues,
Or the sweet-smelling addictive medicinal herb of your words,
May I be able to hold them in my hands,
Feel the air in my lungs and the breath at my nostrils,
And soak in the invigorating fragrance of your loving care.

To Demi
From Yonas"

She loved the tenacious blossom of flowers and always kept a vase on her dresser. Sometimes letting it stay till it all died off, at which point she would flip the upside-down. "They look so pretty dried and curled up!" she would say, smiling from cheek to cheek as though she had invented something novel and brilliant. "Don't let google and YouTube fool you" I would respond jokingly. "You've got to throw them away when they die." These were fresh and air was perfumed by the heavy scent of the lilies. A myriad of vibrant colors evoked the aroma of summers past and transported her to beautiful evenings spent in the arms of the one whom her new flowers were from.

Her smile grew, and her heart erupted in excitement. She wanted to run, she wanted to shout and tell everyone what just happened, but she had to wait, she could only enjoy this alone at the moment, and that was okay. In that moment, the anticipation of being together grew in a manner that is more than words, in a manner that is so tangible. Her focus was poignant as she was filled with anticipation of the trip, she had been talking about with me and planning. So excited, even giddy.

She called me joyfully on video call as happy as a

calm at the high tide or a kitty in a cream pie.

"Oh my gosh, Yonas!" she said as her emotions shone on her face. "These are so beautiful! Thank you so much, I love them!"

"I'm so glad they made it to you," I responded, feeling proud of my accomplishments and the joy I had managed to give her. We spent the rest of the evening on the phone discussing the details of her upcoming trip and how we might react to seeing each other for the first time.

CHAPTER THREE

ßße

BE MY WOMAN

My cell phone buzzed with a text message and two picture attachments. The ID read "Demi" (with a music note and open book emoji next to it). I had given her those emojis as a reminder of how sophisticated our conversations were. A book for the intellectual she is, and a music note for our mutual love of music. I immediately opened the text, my eyes widening, and my face tilting down as I raised the phone in anticipation. The last time I had spoken to Demi before that text was four hours prior, and before that, the previous night. We had been on the phone all through the night talking about the trip, what she would need to pack, her playlist for the plane ride, and what to expect once they arrived…and about how we would react the moment we first saw each other.

I glowed from the inside out—I just had a great

feeling about the day and the upcoming trip. Nothing that ever felt this right could possibly ever go negatively. When I opened Demi's text, I was right, it had two photos attached. One was a selfie with Demi and Jean in the frame, and the other was of the view from inside the airplane along with the words, "We're en route!" and two smiley face emojis.

My heartbeat fast in excitement. She was really coming; it was really happening. In the midst of my inner celebration, another text came in—a photograph of two books stacked on the seat next to Demi, and in the background, on the seats across the aisle, I could see Jean and remember her words. She looked excited to be on the trip as well, and judging by my previous interactions and conversations; her main concern was accompanying Demi to see a guy she'd only known in the digital world and never seen—she couldn't let her make it a solo mission. Good sisters.

Here I had a young lady who, as far the unwritten laws of love are concerned, I would count or call a girlfriend, even though unofficial. We spoke a lot, shared a lot with each other, including secret and personal things, and kept up with each other's lives pretty well. Demi was a decent girl, raised exceptionally well by what I perceived as respectable parents, and was a young Christian girl who wouldn't assume anything and, by her own words and actions, "wasn't in a hurry to jump into anything either." We esteemed each other and understood the boundaries; we edified each other and always sought to restore the other to a place of dignity, peace, and pure joy.

My plan was simple: the very moment I set my eyes on Demi, that very same day—it didn't have to be the same hour or moment, but the same day—I would ask her to date me. I didn't care or want to think much of what our future would look like or how to build it. She had waxed and waned off all that callousness in my heart and my indifference to a relationship. She brought warmth and excitement as I had never experienced before. If anything, even if she were to say no or I, for whatever reason, maintained my ground and kept these growing thoughts and feelings to myself, I would still be all right and happily enjoy the benefits of such an awesome friendship.

It was just past 6:00 AM, and the sun was rising over the city as its rays illuminated the huge pearly outer walls of Union Station D.C. Three American flags danced high in the wind as it teased a cool morning. The forecast called for a high of 78 degrees, making for a great outdoor day. Massachusetts Avenue was just as busy as ever, even on this early Saturday morning, with backed-up traffic of cabs and Uber cars for miles as folks were getting dropped off and awaiting their rides. Jean and Demi were at the end of the line, down the street in a black truck, their Lyft ride from the airport to the station where we would finally meet for the first time, inching down the road in that bumper to bumper traffic at the total maximum speed of about six mph. I had gotten there about twenty minutes early, partially out of sheer excitement and somewhat out of courtesy, so they would not have to sit around waiting for me after a long flight. This was the first time we would all see each other in person, especially exciting for Demi and me. I had known this person for over three great years at this point, and even considered her a best friend, but had never physically set my eyes on her nor physically been in her presence. I couldn't have been more angsty, and Demi, I imagined, couldn't have been more skittish. We stayed on the phone the whole time as I was directing them on where to wait as I approached.

I don't know what souls are made of, but it was instantly clear to me that our souls were made of the same fabric. I had never in my entire life seen melanin so dark and beautiful! This was God's best creation. A queen for the advocacy she possessed. Beauty falls short at capturing what my eyes were beholding, and I could sense care, a love, and support that my soul longed for, but didn't yet know it needed. The moment they stepped out of that bus and I saw Demi standing there, waving back at me from a distance, I had absolutely no doubt in my heart this was going to be the woman I would spend the rest of my existence with, and she would definitely mother my children. Demi's radiance engulfed Jean's and everybody else in that motor park, so much so that I hardly noticed them standing there and could only see her.

"Alright! I think we can go now," shouted Jean, slicing through the moment I just had with Demi. It must have been about only a dozen seconds I stood there starring at her motionless, but it felt like an eternity, and hearing Jean's call snapped me back.

"Welcome to the city, y'all!" I exclaimed, excitedly greeting them with hugs and proceeding to load in their suitcases in the trunk of my Toyota Camry.

Jean immediately climbed in the back seat as Demi hesitated for a quick minute with me at the trunk, almost as if she wanted a minute for just herself and me. We hugged again and, after a brief stare into each other's eyes, accompanied by smiles, she went around to the passenger's seat while I climbed into the driver's side, and off we went.

"So, this is you! Yonas, in the flesh!" Demi said as she stared earnestly at the right side of my face, smiling just enough to not come off to her friends as overly elated at the moment.

The conversations in the car and excited welcomes carried us just far away enough from the busy streets of the station to the heart of the city, where we decided to take advantage of being downtown, find parking, and get a good look at the museums, monuments, sites, and scenes. The intention was to head back up to Maryland later that afternoon, where we would meet up with Jin Rari and O.G., who had also cleared their weekend schedules to welcome the girls to the city and help me in making the weekend as fun and memorable for them as we could.

I've always felt that the best dates happen when you ask someone in the spur of the moment. Going out with the sole purpose and intent of meeting girls and asking them out just hasn't always been my thing. I'm more of a traditionalist who still believes in wooing a woman, who finds importance and value in the power of words and physical presence. I believe in having a conversation that clearly states my intentions and plans for her life, mine, and ours as a unit. In this case, she was present, I was present, and so were our friends, relishing the company of each other like a perfect family reunion filled with great food, games, laughter, and good company. We'd spent a few hours exploring the city, and the night was fast approaching. The sun was setting as a pale tint of orange covered the town, the type that demanded you stop for a snap and an inspiration quote for Social media. It was a bright and serene evening, and so was my mental and emotional state.

I invited Demi to extend the evening and take a walk with me around the town center, where we sat fellowshipping over chicken burritos with our beloved friends. It was a walk around the park like no other.

With each stride, my mind becoming more transparent and more resolute. It was beginning to get dark as the impending night teased the sky into twilight. Curiosity sat slowly on her face as she wondered why I called her away from our gathering with our friends on a sole mission. The boulevard was sentient, living, through the trees and the through people, as if they were in a conversation of some sort, one of sentiments. It was as though the sounds and colors, the movements, and the still spaces, were thousands of weaved moments, both transient and real.

Her eyes were plastered on me. The setting sun painted bright red on her cheeks, caressing her skin, promising new dawn, a new beginning, as the wind shifted her hair around purposefully.

With great detail and clarity of words, I expressed a deep attraction to her and a genuine desire to have her as my girlfriend, if she would let me court her with intent to marry her and father her children. I had only been in her presence for a day, which was enough to confirm everything I had known about her virtually from our Twitter DM days to email, to FaceTime seasons. This was, in fact, the one I would spend the rest of my life with, and I was positively sure of it. A walk that will forever change the trajectory of both our lives.

"Yonas, I have never had a guy ask me out like this. You're so sweet," she responded with a mighty blush blooming across her cheeks.

Her heart was overwhelmed with happiness and appreciation; both expressed in her wide eyes staring straight back at mine with a smile that carried every word out of her beautiful lips with grace. I knew this was what she wanted and would want nothing more than to affirm and commence this journey with me. But she herself was a lady of virtue and principles, who had synchronized her life goals with God's plan and vision for her. She wasn't going to make this decision lightly".

"I would like some time to think it over and get back to you," she requested, adding that we let the rest of our weekend and time together run its course.

She wanted me to let her return home with her thoughts, and a request to pray over it and seek counsel from mentors and spiritual leaders about making the commitment. Nothing could be more attractive than this, a woman who is after God's heart, who wishes to move according to his will and proceed with caution.

"How long do you need?" I inquired, frightened at the thought that she might leave me hanging for months and still possibly return with a negative response.

"Not more than two weeks," she promised and assured me she would not take the matter lightly and was thankful we had this conversation, especially at this time.

It indeed was a beautiful night, capped by a pleasant conversation with an alluring woman. Yes, I was a little nervous at what her response would be, but at the same time, confident in the power of my prayer and the God in whom I trust and serve. Shorty was about to be my wife. It was going to happen.

Over two weeks had passed without her giving me an answer back, all while we carried on our relationship as it stood as healthy. I didn't press of asking her about it much as I waited, confidence in the fact that from the night she took off in the airbus leaving Baltimore for Houston to this moment, she was still thinking of me.

I finally rang her up and brought up the topic during a phone conversation on day twenty, which is when I was pleased to learn she was eager to begin this journey with me, a journey we both knew would someday culminate in matrimony. "of course, I would love to take our relationship to the next level Yonas" she said, prompting me to grin as I dreamt of a life together with Demi sans the distance and need to communicate only via cellular devices.

CHAPTER FOUR

~ॐ~

IPADE AWỌN OBI Rẹ

It's Sunday afternoon and the time is about 2:00 PM. The sun is shining brightly over the suburban neighborhood of Houston, as kids play at the playground with their parents standing by watching. Adjacent to the playground is a cul-de-sac, with five brown brick single-family houses, perfectly lined up, one beside the other. The house sitting at the center of the circle stands out, with unique colors and styling. Inside, the television sits flat, wide, and high on the wall in the living room. Mr. Adebiyi, Demi's father, sits on the couch, keenly watching the CNN news broadcast blaring from the surround sound system. Mrs. Eniola, his wife, is just a few feet away in the kitchen, chopping vegetables at the giant kitchen island, getting ready to make her signature salad. She is preparing a feast. They both knew that Demi would be bringing home a certain young man from out of town for them to meet, but the main focus of this day is the welcoming of their daughter from Nigeria, as they hadn't seen her in several years. They aren't sure exactly what to expect from this friend Demi is bringing home, but know he is someone she is very interested in. Although the significance of it demands their attention to the matter, the main focus is the homecoming of their daughter shortly after.

On the other side of town Demi, and I had just walked out of church service. It was time to put aside all the fun of fellowshipping with fellow believers after excellent service and face the business of our day and weekend together. Bringing me over to her parents' house was no easy task for Demi, nor was it for me as we would have to repeat this Baltimore with my family. We knew what we were against on both ends as the nature of our union not accepted or tolerated in our cultures. "I don't want to see any girl in this house who is not Kenyan!" my mother, Makena, often warned. To which I mostly responded with laugh presuming, she was just expressing her preferences and didn't mean those words or beliefs. After all, I thought to myself, I'm a grown man and can find for myself the best partner, regardless of her country or tribe of origin.

For me, I had a sense of calm about the matter, but this was purely from my naturally unfazed character. We both didn't know exactly what to expect, but we were sure it wasn't going to be an easy task ahead of us. The ride over was as usual—I drive, she rides shotgun, our favorite tunes softly flowing out of the speakers as we chat about things. We enjoyed talking to each other, and always embraced the moment, relishing our physical presence, for seeing each other came with a plane ticket price tag. We would only get to enjoy seeing each other once every two to three months. It would be another long while before I could hold her hand and look into her eyes, and I wasn't going to let the thought of facing her parents stop me from being present and enjoying her company.

We arrived at the house and walked up and into the front door.

"Good afternoon, uncle!" I greeted prostrating to the floor in the customary fashion we are known to give our elders. I had to put my best foot forward at all times. First impressions matter.

"Ehn hen. Afternoon," Mr. Adebiyi replied, with his head tilted down and his chin pressed into his chest as he stared at me through the top of his glasses that hung low on his nose. He must have looked at me for 15 seconds, a mighty long time, staring from the crown of my head to the soles of my feet, as if sizing me up. I immediately turned around to greet Mrs. Eniola, the woman I was hoping would someday be my mother-in-law. I couldn't screw this up. Again, my best foot had to be the leading foot.

"Good afternoon, Mah," I said, bowing down in a similar sign of respect and honor.

The smile on her face died faster than curls of smoke disappearing after a candle flame has been snuffed out. It was like a flashback. The reaction I have seen from my mother Makena whenever I spoke of Demi or proposed to invite her over for a meet. "How are you?" Mrs. Eniola murmured, scanning me from the crown of my head to the sole of my feet and then turning her focus to Demi and proceeded to have a conversation in Yoruba. I couldn't understand a single word or phrase but could discern it wasn't a pleasant one based on the tone. Surely this was what my friend Tayo and many other people I had only heard of till this point endured. Like a scene from the Nollywood movies when the dear mother is discerning for her son or daughter who the stranger is that stands before them with interest to their offspring. Their brows cave inwards as their eyes open wide with every word over-pronounced, slicing rather than tumbling through the dry air, creating creases on their lips and forehead. I had seen it in my mother, and I was living it again here. Enough to squeeze every ounce of hope you have of gaining a foot in. But our evening was far from over.

The conversation was stale. Our purpose was unwelcomed, yet scarcely fair at all, I thought. I could tell this wasn't normal for Demi. She felt apologetic and awkward. But it was alright; we'd discussed this. We had an idea of what to expect and how to respond. I found a divergent in engaging in some "man talk" with Mr. Adebiyi, during which I was flooded with questions about my background, my occupation, family history, my education, my intentions, and my ambitions. A myriad of questions each one following the other like bullets from an automatic rifle. I never really got the chance to answer any single question adequately, as the minute I began a response, I was cut short by another question on a whole different topic. It all came to a screeching halt when the doorbell rang, and in came Demi's the long-awaited sister—saved by the bell. She was full of energy and happy for a person who had just stepped off a 22 hours flight. It was a relief for the pressure Demi, and I had been under.

Food was soon ready to be served, and we all gathered around the table for a brief word of prayer, led by Mr. Adebiyi, after which we sat down to eat. All the while, I had been going back and forth, joining in conversations between Mr. Adebiyi and his son, engaging in one-on-one conversations with the wife, and even trying to help in the kitchen where Demi and her mother had been cooking. Yet, I was never able to break into the bonding, always feeling out of place and unwanted. Demi could sense it; our business here wasn't going so well or remotely as we had imagined. I was never asked what my purpose for being there was, not even at the dinner table, also though Demi's sister introduced the idea with light jokes, which unfortunately fell flat to a silent reaction. Not a grin, not a comment.

Hours had passed, and darkness had set in. It was time for me to make my exit, but I couldn't just leave without having a shot at stating my case. I believed I needed to be heard—I certainly didn't deserve to be heard but felt I had earned the right to have the conversation I wanted to have. It was time to at least properly introduce myself. I knew, of course, that it wouldn't make any sense to say, "I am here to formally introduce myself as Demi's friend," I explained with my knees buckling in anxiety. Just fried was enough. Friend! Girlfriend would never fly in my own house, as I would be greeted with a slap, so I expected the same standard here and knew the verbal boundaries. My desire to make it be known that our relationship was intense and very serious was there, but the opportunity was always absent. Before I could execute, however, I was summoned by Mr. Adebiyi, to a private quarter of the house, and in a brief lecture, was warned off.

"Young man, I know why you have come here," he said. "Demi has been telling us about you, and I want to let you know personally that you have done well in respecting our culture and coming to see me, but we cannot allow whatever relationship you two have to carry on. You are both still young and have a full life ahead of you. We do not support this, and I suggest you two talk about it and end the relationship as soon as possible. Do you understand?" He demanded.

"Yes sir," I responded, understanding his tone and choice of words but feeling the reality of it deep in the soul.

He asked me to promise I would break up with Demi and leave her alone. I had never been this stuck in my life. This was her father, a person she'd looked up to her whole life, asking me to leave his daughter alone. As a man, this is the person whose respect and admiration you seek the most while doing these kinds of hand in marriage, asking things. A clear and final mandate, there wasn't any room for any doubt. I was to get out of the picture and far away from the family and Deme.

Still, I wasn't about to betray our future and our plans. At least not this easy or fast. I had some faith that as a man, I would be able to reason with him in time. I figured if I could just explain and show him how much I cared about his daughter and how I would work hard to make sure she was happy. If we could let this breathe, come home and win over my side and my family, then surely, we could all be one happy multi-cultural African family someday.

We exited the house, and into the car we went,

driving off to where I lodged for the weekend. My flight home was a red-eye flight, and we had a lot to consider. A lot to think about pertaining to our future and endeavors. The ride back was unlike the trip before. The silence in the car was deafening. We were both heartbroken and saddened. Admittedly, I need another shot, I thought to myself. Maybe Mrs. Eniola had a different opinion. If I could win over Makena for us, I would win over my father. If I could win Mrs. Eniola for us, regardless of her demeanor during the evening, I could win over Mr. Adebiyi. Our mothers have a soft spot on their hearts that only need to be searched with tender care and patience. It wasn't impossible.

I whipped the car around, explaining to Demi we were going back, to seek a word with her mother. She was torn between admiration for my bravery and fear of the outcome.

We pulled up in the driveway, and back into the house, we went. I respectfully requested to speak with Mrs. Eniola in private, hoping to plead our case and get a different reaction, or at least try to win her over so she could petition her husband for our sake. She pulled me to a private corner of the house with Demi just a few feet away, with angst visible in her face, listening in anticipation of how this dialogue was going to play out.

"Aunty?" I said, as is the traditional manner of addressing a woman of her stature.

And before I opened my mouth to utter a word, I was stopped with a pointed warning finger. The words that followed cut deep to the marrow of my bones.

"We would rather not accept any young man other than Yoruba or Nigerian in our family. Or a husband to Demi. You are a respectable young man for coming to us first before doing anything, but we it cannot happen. We have welcomed you with grace and peace, but this should be the last time you return here, and the last time you see Demi!" she concluded.

I had heard of this happening to others. Tayo sitting across from me in his living room, listening to my account was only a few years fresh out of his battle. But to joy, his bride was his in their happy home despite remnants of the fight they still dealt with.

Sadly, this was only our beginning as we had a promise to be among the triumphant, but the second leg was in Baltimore at another date with another set of parents to wrestle with.

CHAPTER FIVE

⁓ꝋꝋℓ⁓

MOVING ON IS HARDER

In the aftermath of that unsuccessful dinner, meeting Demi's family felt like a huge mistake on both our part. We beat ourselves up for weeks, wondering how differently we could have approached the situation, if we made a move too prematurely, or if we'd ever get another fair shot. It was inevitable that I would have had to meet them at some point, that she would have to meet my folks at some point. But how different would the outcome have been if we waited, or if we eased into it? How different would it have been if we tried my side first? It felt rushed, it felt early, it felt unplanned. Regret and doubt sad heavy on us for days after. We blew it, and there wasn't any fixing it.

I had never understood why love needed to be free, but I did, at this point, at least to some degree. Were we to relive the moment, I would try to summon more counsel from Tayo, or maybe even O.G., or someone who could help, but I wouldn't have gone into the meeting based only on the feeling of the power of love. I failed myself, and Demi too. I was tired of thinking about it, but no amount of analysis could turn back the clock and give us another shot. I had to get on with the here and now, to be able to make a better choice if ever I got another shot. And I couldn't help but wonder how many people around the world, or from my community, had walked in my shoes? I thought of Tayo and the other stories I had heard of growing up

It's a problem that is probably as old as time, and not unique or distinctive to Demi and I. Shakespeare conferred enduring fame on it in his romantic tragedy Romeo and Juliet. Jerry Bock's 1964 Broadway musical Fiddler on the Roof embodied it as a central theme. Julian Fellowes's 2019 hit Downton Abbey also explores this theme—the struggle of the parent generation to accept their adult children's choices. As timeless and universal the matter maybe, when it comes home, it's agonizing.

When your family or beloved parents, the ones who raised you and whose respect and love you treasure, disapprove of your partner...where do you turn?

*****

There are millions of people in love. They each want their family to respect and love the person they've chosen to spend their life with. But sometimes, loved ones cannot always see past misplaced prejudices, traditions, and values. The thought of it baffled me. I had become my reality. My girlfriend and sweetheart, as amazing a person as she was, there was a very high probability my family would be blind to it, only seeing her as an outsider, someone who will never fit in with the family culture. I knew bridging this divide that has crippled relationships and marriages for centuries can only be accomplished with clear intentions, commitment, and the compromises Demi and myself were willing to make to stay together. I had only heard of it, but now come to experience it and could only imagine the constant rejection and disapproval from one or both sides that would manifest itself through intense but unexpressed anger, seething under the surface of passive-aggressive words and despicable actions.

This constant push and pull undermines relationships and can put a couple in a dreadful bind. Heeding and responding to either side, the family or your partner, makes you feel disrespected or abandoned. As a partner, you will always feel the pressure of having to prove yourself to be worthy because you are the focus of dislike. These efforts can quickly turn into resentment and anger toward the love of your life, which can spill into a tragic breakup of a beautiful relationship.

The pendulum can swing, from a less dramatic situation to verbal abuse and threats, or even deadly ones, where lives have been lost from physically violent attacks. The solutions vary as well, and fortunately, there are the solutions that don't result in the tragic ending seen in Romeo and Juliet. "do you think they might change their mind once we have kids?" I sometimes asked Demi, thinking of days when everything might be bliss. Because there are families who eventually accept their adult children's choices, and even give their full sincere blessings. Maybe all it takes is patience, hard work, and willingness, however, and doesn't happen by magic or by argument. Then, there are those whose battle has more twists, turns, and detours. Demi and I were part of that unfortunate second bunch.

*****

Music had been my love for many years. I always found complete joy and happiness being in the studio writing and recording songs or being on stage performing in front of an audience. As an African who was raised in a culture that places such a high value on education, I worked just as hard to attain the highest level of education and secure a stable career post-graduation. All this I did, not because I was forced to, but because I enjoyed the pursuit. Whenever I was asked about my goals in life, in addition to achieving success, be it in music or the work world, I always added the desire to have a wife and kids who all will be there with me to enjoy the fruits of my labor.

Thoughts and dreams I had never let anyone into before meeting Demi. In the three years that we shared a typical friendship, she had watched me wrestle with my fears, hone my craft, dream, and dream all over again. She had graduated from merely aiding in seeing a young black king pursue his passion, to actively participating in the hustle and grind, watching me draw close to that goal line. She had both hands on the wheel, celebrating every milestone, and trusting every step of the process. I had always dreamt of leading a house that didn't feel like the one I grew up in, and Demi was the perfect match for me in building that home.

Although our relationship was mostly lived through long-distance, over video calls and lengthy text messaging chats that lasted all day, I held her hand through her openness and the trust she had for me. I hugged her through her kindness and expression of godly womanhood, which drew me in all the more to want to be with her. We'd become so close yet separated by many miles.

How could a parent not see or understand the happiness of a daughter or who had come face to face with a genuine and wholesome partner? How could they not give me a chance, or at least get to know a person before writing him or her off? These were questions that we didn't know would plague us for the rest of our lives. However, one thing was for certain, and it was that Mr. Adebiyi and Mrs. Eniola's along with Makena's and every family or parent prejudice of foreigners and the union of union two cultures or relationship is just a manifestation of their lack of empathy, fear, and insecurities.

Our happiness didn't exist and wasn't a considering factor in both families. They buried our joy with my own hands, deep into the soil, eyes closed without care. This prejudice masqueraded as an ointment to hurt was in all truth more than fuel for the flames that scorch hundreds of beautiful unions like the one Demi, and I had. More loathing only guaranteeing more division, more pain. Never more healing or an increase in our humanity and diversity as two compatible people from two corners of the world become one in love. Surely if we fought it till the end or till the death of us, it wouldn't be passed like a dark flame from one generation to the next.

Demi and I, we had been dating for almost a year before making that bold first move to meet with her family. We continued pursuing our relationship with counsel, much prayer, and cautiousness for months, even though the demand was to cease speaking to and seeing each other with immediate effect. Their reasons could not have been more out of line with what we believed biblically or culturally. Their ideas were based solely on what I think is an intense or irrational dislike or fear of people from other countries or cultures due to illogical fears, close-mindedness, and cultural myths.

My presence in Demi's home that day had brought into her life a virus that would plague us and disrupt the trajectory of what could be the rest of our life. Imagine a young woman raised in a wholesome loving home with both parents, loved and provided for. The bond and relationship a daughter and her mother had, so strong, almost sister-like, very admirable. But with Mrs. Eniola not at all liking the idea of her daughter dating or considering marrying a guy, not from Nigeria, it tore at Demi, though it didn't affect how she felt about me or how I felt about her. To protect such a bond under these circumstances, conversations became painfully limited and hidden. Visits became less frequent and stealthy. Demi couldn't be caught on the phone talking to me. I couldn't mention her name around my folks. They weren't having it. The instruction was that clear and strictly enforced. I couldn't be seen with her. She wasn't welcomed over. We secretly booked trips and flew out to visit each other. We fought back, fighting for the right to love, always believing that "they will come around shortly," as many advised us.

The pressure from home did not cease or ease up for Demi, however, and with that growing pressure, especially being a young girl trying to balance the hustles of life and responsibilities, there was only so much she could do, especially when trying to honor her mother and maintain peace within the family. We often wondered and questioned if we went about meeting the right way, questioning if we should have waited, or taken different steps, or slowed down the introduction, etc. This also prevented us from bringing our relationship to the attention of my own parents. It made no sense to move forward with such plans or any other plans when the future of our togetherness was beginning to be in question. My family was ultimately in the dark as to who I was seeing and what I was going through, though they had an idea that I was in a relationship with a girl of whom I was very fond. All the while, as things were increasingly growing rocky at home for Demi, our conversations became frustratingly and exclusively centered around how to move forward.

Losing Demi was out of the picture for me. I could not picture myself without her. This is why I promised her I would fight, even till the very end, to keep our relationship alive and marry her, despite all the odds we faced. She was fair, virtuous, wise, and though just one woman, shame came with all grace. Nobody is perfect, but she was perfect for me. And yet, I could not see a way forward for us. Increasingly, it seemed to me that the end was drawing near.

Of course, I knew losing my beloved would mean many more years spent single, or in the dating parlor, lingering, but with no intent, real prospect, or desire to marry. Many more years of trails of broken hearts left behind, be it maliciously or unintended. Being left empty-handed because love had once been stolen from me. But then again, maybe truly the Lord gives, and He also takes away, and if I were to become single and stay single, it would be my pride that kept me in that position because the hard-working, extroverted, exotic, beautiful, humorous, intelligent, and Christian woman I preferred just doesn't exist. I would be standing, so unbendable on my preferences, that the world around me would question if the good Lord has yet created such a woman. Ignoring every good girl who would show interest because of my great expectations of whom I ought to be with, resisting any rumors of interests and revisiting thoughts of Demi, only to be left with endless "what if?" questions.

Our relationship was sort of still in a very safe and early stage (other than the reactions from our families), although I had made it plain to Demi that my intention was to one day marry her. Her intense love and loyalty to her family, however, and the immense pressure from her mother made it nearly impossible to enjoy the relationship at this stage, or endure the constant fights and quarrels, especially with me being hundreds of miles away with no tangible means to protect and support her in the event she loses her family to disownment, which were some of the threats.

We wanted to do things the proper way and not go behind our families or against the counsel of those who poured into us, but seek all the right approvals along the way as we worked through this dating phase into what we anticipated would be courtship, then, eventually, culminating in marriage. I looked back and beat myself up, knowing this was probably the biggest mistake that put us in the situation we were in. It was my idea for Demi to inform her parents, or at least make them aware, that she was talking to a guy in Baltimore who was from Kenya, and she had a serious interest in pursuing a long-lasting relationship with him.

Of course, this was just a tap on the gas pedal, not a full-throttle approach, as I didn't want to come off too strong and direct to begin with. Demi and I had shared conversations of the possibility of a serious push back from both sides of our family but always trusted in the sovereignty of God and the prospect of them coming around, if not once we got engaged, God willing, when our children (and their grandchildren) started showing up. I mean, who would want to miss out on their grandchild's life, right? Or miss out on being involved in their daughter's or son's wedding? I figured, if it worked for others, it certainly can work for us too, with a lot of prayer, consistency, and patience.

Well, Mrs. Eniola and Mr. Adebiyi had other plans, and so did my family, as they immediately knocked down the idea and warned Demi to call off the relationship while it was still early and while she still had their favor. This wasn't a phone conversation I had ever anticipated that I would have, in all my years of existence.

The phone rang at about 5:36 PM, and it was Demi calling. She didn't sound too pleasant, and I already knew it was going to be one of those nights. She tried desperately to mask the panic in her voice, but I knew her too well to be fooled.

"Yonas, I need you! I can't do this on my own up here, it's too much, I need you!" she pleaded.

"Babe, I'm so sorry. What's wrong? What happened!?" I asked, trying to console her and assure her I was there, and her comfort was with me.

My attitude in response to calls like this always defined what happened after. I could meet the challenge with humility, grace, and calm, or do the opposite. It was never easy. Each time seemed more significant and important than the previous occurrence, as the urgency had escalated.

We had been texting earlier throughout the day, as I was the only one, she could talk to who wasn't hounding her about our relationship. I was the only one who could just make her feel loved again, or who could help ease the pressure.

Our relationship was still at a very early stage, and though I knew it would absolutely break Demi's heart,

I was somewhat okay with dropping the dating title and idea of courtship or even marriage for a long while, and just focusing on staying distant friends while we figured out a means to conquer this red tape, for the sake of tranquility. I was scared. Terribly scared. I had been there for Demi many times and won. Saved and comforted her over and over...but this time the forces against our relationship seemed to have me outgunned.

The conversation was somber, and often filled with long periods of silence. Not because we didn't know what to say to each other, but just because of the overwhelming nature of the situation.

"I never asked you to defend yourself, babe," I said, cutting through the silence. "I love the peace-lover and pacifist that you are, but please, please, you have to open your eyes and realize what is coming!"

"What are you talking about, Yonas!" she hollered, disappointed, and surprised at my attitude and response to her plight.

If attacking everything we loved meant stopping us from seeing each other, they would. It was clear and evident. I wouldn't bury my head in the sand. I saw it coming and thought we didn't have too much skin in the game to stay locked in. Getting out of the line of fire was a viable option, and convincing Demi was the next step.

CHAPTER SIX

RISKY

I swung the door open inwards as I walked in, exhausted from a tiresome day at the office. Still catching my breath and recovering from climbing the one step it takes to get into my house, I flung my keys on the kitchen table while bracing myself for my next challenge: the flight of stairs that led straight into my bedroom. I'm about to fall flat on that bed and pass out for at least the next two hours, I thought to myself, much anticipating that long-awaited nap. However, before I could take another step, my phone suddenly buzzed in my pocket, sending me into a state of irritation at why anyone would want to cut into my nap time.

Even though responding to this message was the last thing on my mind, I knew I couldn't ignore this particular message because it came from Demi. Three strong vibrations (with the last one having a bit of a draw to it) was the unique setting I had assigned Demi, alongside a special ringtone that let me know she was calling without me having to check to see.

"We need to talk about who the hell is this girl in your snaps, Yonas," the message read. I stood there, my thoughts racing back and forth in all four corners of my brain as I pondered in utter confusion and panic. Why would she send me such a text message after not having spoken to me for the last several months? Our falling out was so strong that we couldn't even be casual friends or mates after that recent conversation we had. We had chosen to keep our distance from each other, cutting off any form of communication to aid in the healing we needed after the breakup, and receiving this message came as an absolute bombshell.

A sudden rush of energy came over me. Whatever plan I had to rest was out the window. This was a serious business that needed my immediate attention. I quickly dialed Demi's number to try and make sense of this, to figure out where she was coming from, or at least get a chance to explain exactly what the heck I was doing with Liz.

I had been talking to Liz all day via text. Our relationship had been casual. Speak here, speak there, we only knew each other in passing as a friend of a friend. I had gotten to know Liz, much like Demi, through social media. She very aesthetic and always had on the freshest and newest pair of sneakers. A cool young lady like such who is always well dressed in the latest and exclusives will but commanded or attract attention in whatever circle she stood in. Her smooth and fair skin could not be missed when she walked into a room. She always had a broad smile that covered her face displaying her bright white teeth.

I somehow got it in my head that she would be a great companion for my O.G. After all, he was looking, and I could hook my guy up if it would work out. He was a great guy. Mostly shy and reserved but charming and funny when comfortable. O.G. was a darker-skinned, nicely built guy who always kept a perfectly lined up goatee. He always lit up at the sight of a good-looking, fair, young lady, such as Liz. "Shorty bad son! And she fair too! Ouuuu!" he would say, shaking his head with a smile that stretched from ear to ear. Liz was just the right one for him, though he didn't know it yet. I would go on about how great it would be if he and Liz gave a relationship a try.

However, O.G. scoffed at the idea, shooting down all my aspirations and dreams. He justified it with his disdain for long-distance relationships, plus he already had plans to pursue a young lady he'd been talking.

Being the single young lady that she was, Liz enjoyed traveling and had DC on her radar. With Demi now out of my life for the time being, and without the luxury of speaking with her daily like I was used to, I found myself talking to other friends and family more and more. Liz had become one of my close friends. I always pride myself in having the heart to check on people and not rely only on social media for updates. I enjoy a good conversation over the phone, or via text messaging, and knowing how to sustain a good friendship has always been a strong suit of mine.

They say after a breakup, the guy tends to move on more quickly, while the girl endures the hurt for a longer period of time. Or maybe as guys, we tend to find some sort of comfort or refuge in pursuing other pleasures in a way that acts as a distraction and camouflages our hurt. Whatever it is, I found myself talking to and hanging out with a lot more friends than I usually would, and Liz was one of them.

The pain and hurt from the rejection Demi and I received was agonizing enough and unbearable to begin to build with somebody else. I was utterly numb to my feelings, yet trying to nurture and cater to the tastes of another person. Too crushed and devastating that I had promised myself, I would never entertain another long-distance relationship and was sticking by that conviction no matter what. I had, in a sense, partially reverted back to my old ways of not giving a care about what a female wants. In my mind, mostly, I desired to stay relationship-free. But no matter how hard life hits and how secluded you want to be from people, courtesy and kindness is always a good thing. I can't turn the homie down on a good time in my city, I thought to myself, when Liz informed me, she was planning a trip from her hometown Ohio and was very interested in seeing DC for a day, provided I show her around. I loved the idea and offered to take her on tour. She was all in, and tickets were booked.

The day Liz came down, it was bright and sunny, and the city was full of sightseeing tourists from all over the world, taking pictures with loved ones in front of monuments, or smiling from their seats as they rolled by on the topless tour buses. The night before, I had mapped out what spots we were going to hit, what exactly we were going to see, who we'd link up with, and when, because it was a day trip and time was precious. I picked Liz up and off we went, first to the Washington monument, where she took lots of pictures, and then a stroll to 1600 Pennsylvania Ave NW to see the White House. I mean, who doesn't want a picture at the White House? That's sure to get you 100 Social Media likes in under a minute, especially for somebody who is from way out of town! She'd been doing Snapchat the whole time, wherever we went, and the more she did snaps, the more I didn't mind being in one or maybe a couple. For the most part, though, I was content to either be behind the camera, helping take some dope shots or stepping aside for the snaps.

But, lo and behold—the White House! I mean, it was the freaking White House, occupied by President

Barack Obama. I hadn't been there in a while, and dang it, I just had to flex one time for the gram. I grabbed a photo with Liz and posted it on my social. Then another group selfie and then a video, all of which gave off the vibe of us having a perfect time.

The day continued on, we linked up with O.G. as planned, grabbed some lunch, then he dropped Liz at the train station and off to Ohio she returned. Like clockwork, much to my absolute surprise, the very minute I got home my cell phone began ringing. It was Demi. I hadn't seen or heard from her in months! Demi and I hadn't spoken in almost a year, and I was particularly nervous that she wanted to discuss Liz. Surely, she'd seen the posts, and I was most definitely in some trouble. After all, a break, at least the nature of ours, doesn't mean freedom to galivant around town and share it without any regards.

The phone kept ringing as if it would never be stopped, and finally, I hit the green button, and that radiant voice came through the speaker, and all the feels hit me at ones like an 18-wheeler running into a wall at 90mph.

"Hi Yonas," she said.

Now, I know Demi very well. Even though I hadn't spoken to her in a very long time, some things just never change. Right away, I knew "Hi Yonas" was not a good thing. It never was. Demi would usually come on the phone with a greeting like, "Hi babe," or

"Heyyyy," or whatever else, but whenever I heard "Hi Yonas" with my whole name, it never was a good sign, especially paired with her tone.

I immediately went into small talk mode, being that we had some catching up to do, but she didn't call for that. Things got awkward fast, as I could sense there was something pressing her. I asked what the matter was, and she opened up about how much her phone had been blowing up the past couple of hours with friends calling and texting, sending screenshots, inquiring about how messed up it was that I could move on by going out with a good mutual friend. We all know there are boundaries and rules to this love game, and I got it, I understood precisely how difficult and frustrating it was for her to receive those texts and calls. She didn't deserve that, and I had some explaining to do.

That call turned into a conversation that lasted about three hours and was probably the deepest and most real talk we had ever had. By the end, we both found ourselves in a position of realization—the realization of how much we missed each other; realization of how easily we had let outside influences kill our dreams and hopes; realization of how much potential we had as a couple, how much support we had from friends; and a mutual realization that we had a tough battle ahead of us if we were to pursue the relationship again. If I were in her presence at that very moment, I would have kissed her. A kiss so pure and so bliss because of the peril and pain that had torn us apart. We both understood there was bound to be other fights in the very near future for us—but we were both strong-willed—always coming back in each other's arms that were such heaven that we wondered whether the joy wasn't worth the agony: all the highs and all the lows.

We didn't have a plan. In fact, all we had was a were promises and vows right then and there to renew the relationship and fight for it till the end, till victory was won. We knew what we wanted. And, just like that, I had my girl back. A risky move that turned into a blessing.

CHAPTER SEVEN

This is Us

Tayo, still listening with a warm heart and being curious regarding how to cure with his response and words, saw a man in me who had come face to face with stern rejection rather than the love that sees a sea of emotions within. He, my friend, heard my heart and felt the sadness below rage. I continued my account.

*****

If you believe there is such a thing as a soul mate—"a person ideally suited to another as a close friend or romantic partner," as defined by the dictionary—then I found mine in Demi. Demi made me a better person...well, realistically speaking, she didn't make me a better person, but she inspired and motivated me to be a better person, not just for myself, but for us. A soul mate is someone who you carry with you forever.

It's the one person who knows you, accepts you, and believes in you, even when no one else will. And no matter what happens, you will always love them in some way.

The feelings were mutual between Demi and me—I was her person, and she was mine. My beloved and me. Her family, on the other hand, and mine both thought otherwise. They saw our union as nothing but a threat, using stereotypical horror stories to justify their arguments and deter us from pursuing each other. What exactly could it have been? Was I just a nobody from a no man's land? Did I not have enough wealth to support Demi? Was she not just a human-like any other Kenyan woman? Did I look famished and scraggy? I wasn't man enough, and, most importantly, wasn't Nigerian. And as such, she wasn't Kenyan enough. Makena had in fact, also put her foot down against my dreams and desire.

This fight and clash between cultures and between lovers had been a choreographed dance of ruin for a very long time. It tore us where we need to heal. But the time has come for us to learn some new moves. To put down the arsenal and use empathy. We needed an avenue to communicate our truth to the ones we loved. The truth that had tortured us so that a new and better future could be birth.

*****

There is beauty in learning a new culture, a woman

leaving her father's house and cleaving to her husband's culture, while still maintaining the beauty of the values her mother and folks raised her with. The world is one big melting pot of cultures, and if any man and woman find love in each other and desire to pursue the covenant of marriage together, there shouldn't be any man or woman who stops this union based only on the fact that they are not from the same country or tribe.

It becomes more complicated, however, with two people of different religions, such as Christian and Muslim, for example, who may take their faith seriously in terms of rules regarding marriage and partnerships. As I stated in the preface, one of the reasons why I wrote this book was because not only is my story my power, but I also recognized Demi and I were not the only people who have had to go through such a painful and difficult situation—and neither would we be the last. I understand (in theory) why our families might have been strongly opposed to our associated with each other in any fashion, but their methods were completely asinine, harsh, and illegal, not to mention immoral.

"You need to leave that girl alone or you will not have a place in this family" I was warned by Makena and my folks whose opinion I respected—giving me much to consider as I was now seen as the wayward of the family and a son who wouldn't heed to the family traditions and culture.

"You are trying to split a family, and it is not right!" I was warned by Mrs. Eniola, further stamping our demise and putting red tape all over our hopes and aspirations. When African parents tell you not to do something, you just listen. Period. Even if there is a reasonable reason why.

*****

In Christ, God is creating a new humanity, or you might say a new race, and it is called the Christian race. All races, tribes, and tongues of all nations have one ancestor, Adam, who was created by God in His image, and all humans following from him are in God's image, essentially making it one Godlike human race as we are thought in Genesis 1:27. In Jesus, ethnic and social differences come to an end in being terms of being obstacles to deep, personal, intimate fellowship. Christ is all, and if there was one thing Demi and I shared, it was Christ! "A wife is bound to her husband as long as he lives. But if her husband dies, she is free to be married to whom she wishes, only in the Lord" (1 Corinthians 7:39). There are hundreds, if not thousands, of reasons why it is right to not merely tolerate but to gladly celebrate the union of a godly, Christ-exalting man and woman who are marrying across racial, tribal, and national lines. It will not destroy any God-appointed diversity in the world, but will, in fact, mark that diversity and the power of Christ.

So, when it comes to a soul mate, sometimes we lose love, we make mistakes, and we miss opportunities, but what is meant for you will be for you, and that's that.

Demi was my person, and God brought her to me. One single move beat dark forces and achieved many good things to make our bond possible. We were as greatest lovers and the greatest of soldiers, with a vow to fight for love all our days till the end. The end here didn't just mean a home together with pets, great careers, and children, but rather, till death. Only warriors can have soulmates. Soldiers willing to go all the way through with no half-stepping or retreat when the combat became too onerous. For no perfectly formed words or phrases could do the job, not even the purest intentions, but only actions birthed in the household of bravery and valor. And in a battle like such that we found ourselves in, the worst was yet to come.

CHAPTER EIGHT

~∂∂e~

The Breakup II

She stood about 5 feet and 5 inches tall. She mostly wore her natural black hair slicked back into a ponytail, with an extension that sometimes puffed, and other times the curls hung just above her shoulders. "What do you think?" she would ask in excitement. "Should I do it with curls or straight?" But no matter what my response was, she always resorted to her trusted curls. It never failed her. Her edges lay curled on her forehead, emphasizing the amount of precision and effort it took to achieve this perfection.

She loved to pray. She was always considering others in her prayers and offering up ample thanksgiving for the faithfulness of God. "Lord, I'm grateful that you are sovereign and in control of our situation," she would say. "You have the power to calm the greatest of storms, heal the sick, and resurrect from the dead. 'The king's heart is a stream of water in the hand of the Lord; he turns it wherever he will.'" She adds, "you can certainly change our families' hearts to love and support our union." Softly spoken, with her sweet little subtle voice, so low, almost as if she was whispering, with our eyes closed and heads tilted down if we were on a FaceTime call, or hands locked into each other's if we were privileged to be together on a visit.

I needed this kind of energy in my life. It was hard and difficult life season, like in a bottomless abyss, and her hope and fight, which was more reliable than mine, was like a single blazing match, leading me out from underneath the never-ending dark cloud that consumed me. She gave me hope and fought for our love with every fiber in her body. She gave up sleep for me. She shed tears for us, endured long hours of scolding and estrangement from her family, all for our sake. She was committed and always there, even through the most difficult times, times when my hopes wavered, and all fight in me was depleted.

A real ride or die, a legitimate partner, Demi, was my best friend. I sometimes want to take credit for creating this in her, for this was like a role reversal. Our first breakup after my very first introduction to her family came as a result of her not being fully committed to us. It was much easier to let go then. I saw a whole new world with and in her, and nothing anybody could do or say would have pried me from my commitment to love, provide for, and protect her.

When she was feeling doubtful at the earlier stages of our relationship, when she was unsure and more willing to consider heeding her parent's warnings and demands, I convinced her to believe in us and give us a chance. I gave her assurance that they would come around; if not while we were still courting, then definitely when children came into the picture. I promised her we would be all right, and all she had to do was trust me and know that no matter what, I was going to take us all the way. I didn't convince her of this overnight; it took a few long and challenging months of affirming words and actions that showed her I was reliable and that I could be trusted to protect, pray for, and provide for her.

But now, the tables had turned, and in my seasons of doubt and fear, she was the stronger one. She was the one putting up the fight for us, and though I had skin in the game, my efforts were not as convincing. I was crippled by doubts, fears, and uncertainties, which all caused more stress on our already struggling bond. Day after day of hours and hours of conversations, with back and forth arguments on what we were going to do, also didn't help. One thing was is for certain, our union, though would be a thing of celebration by our generation, was not fathomable by the ages before us. Our struggle alongside the many who found themselves in the similar ordeal was for the joy of securing a better future for the next generation and the beauty of two cultures coming together.

I depended on my ability to provide for her, as a man and as a leader. But the denial from both sides of our family had made a significant dent into our relationship and influenced my outlook on the future. We were both sitting at the table, but my side felt like it was collapsing. We were reading the same book but on different pages. Still, rather than put an end to it, as was the order from everybody we loved and sort support from, we continued on, trying to work through the difficulties and relentless pushback.

"Forget being a couple, let's just focus on working on our friendship," I said to Demi in defeat, without thinking twice about the consequences or effect those words might have on her delicate heart. Déjà vu.

So much pain—deep sighs, long pauses in conversation, crying. Unbearable. I came to the conclusion that I had to let go. We had come to a breaking point, and it was time to call it. We weren't getting any support from either side of our families.

I couldn't deal with the weightiness of the responsibility and duty I had as the man and leader in this relationship. Making the decisions wasn't something I should have done on my own, but in essence, Demi's and my life hung in the balance; our future was dependent on it. The opposite of leaving and cleaving as Genesis 2:24 tells us. Not a leaving and cleaving with celebrations and the joy of having one's family there. But the leaving and cleaving of losing one's family and culture altogether. Everything was crumbling around us. It felt as though I had boulders on my shoulders, and gravity was pulling me down from the cloud nine of love I had known for the past seven years.

I had to let go, for reasons I couldn't even articulate to her, to myself, or to anybody for that matter. But I had to let go. The hatred and the threats from her parents, especially, and from family on both sides, was too much, and her parents were only escalating their threats and demands that I stay away from their precious daughter. Our relationship felt like it was decimating me; my care and passion for Demi was depleting. I had lost all motivation and reason to fight. There was absolutely no joy left—misery was our company, a thick dark cloud hung over our heads. So, though I loved her, though I needed her, I had to let go. We spoke, but we didn't understand each other, and the more we tried, the more we destroyed each other. We loved to the bone but broke like skeletons. Our hearts hung on to hope too long and became delicate.

How did this happen to us? What happened to cultural diversity? How did other people do it? How could we possibly not be meant for each other?

Millions of questions flooded my mind, none of which I could answer, but one thing was for absolute sure: I was a miserable idiot, a damn fool. She loved me to shredded pieces, she was filled with so much fight and purpose, ready to endure for as long as it would take to make things work and come out victorious at the end, but I was too short-sighted and had had enough.

"Yonas, if you leave me now, you can never hit me up again and try to fix this. You are about to let go of a good thing. You should probably pray about this, and we can revisit later. Yonas, I care about you, baby. You are not thinking straight right now. Please, don't do this to us!" she pleaded.

The words hit me paralyzing us to silence like a poison to the bone marrow, and in that void of sound, the shallowness of our exhausted conversation was laid bare. What used to be a grace-filled colloquy of understanding and comedic moments were entirely vapid. It had been years we'd been through it. Everything was a re-hash, recycled. And so, without a star in the sky to lead or a view at the light at the tunnel end, my bags were packed.

My mind was set in. For weeks leading up to this moment, I thought I could not fight the apathy that had grown in me. I had grown apart from Demi. I don't know how long you can fight, but in the end, every soldier gets battle weary. I didn't want to waste her time any longer.

But this time, it was different.

"If we stop now, the future might be different," I emphasized to her.

But deep down, I didn't believe that myself, even though I once did. This time, it was just to end the conversation, even further, to put a complete stop to the nightmare, because nothing else I could say seemed to work in making Demi ease up and let me go. I was truly done. She was hurt, heartbroken, disappointed, shocked, and utterly surprised I would do this to her at such a time and in such a fashion. All the time spent trying to prove myself, not only to her but especially to her parents, left me feeling defeated.

Demi had always hailed me as the greatest, her best ever, her everything, her one in a million, but at that very moment, I felt like nothing. All the time spent trying to prove myself had me feeling faded. I had given my all; I had granted my soul. Demi knew this, she had given the same and so much more, much more than I could ever repay. That's why I had to let go.

The pressure was coming from all directions. In a relationship, if you know what you want and have made promises to yourself and the person you are with that you will achieve a goal, it should be a quest worth pursuing, no matter what. I always knew our story wasn't novel, but it was unique to us. "I promise you, when we make it out of this, we will have the world to tell! We will have the world to inspire!" I would say to

Demi, often accompanied by a kiss to the forehead or a long, tight hug. Even though it felt like a very lonely battle, like we were alone in this with no support, despite prayers and encouraging words from pastors and friends, we were comforted by the fact that we were not the first to ever go through such an ordeal. Coming out, victorious, was imperative for us. After all, in the five years of courting Demi, plus the three years we spent as just friends, I had been seeking out advice from older couples who had gone through similar situations. "Where there is no guidance, a people falls, but in an abundance of counselors, there is safety" (Proverbs 11:14).

This wasn't the making of martyrdom, for I had been stripped of all boldness. The extreme hatred, which put a wedge between my love and me, pushed me further. "I'll take the blame for the both of us," I thought to myself. Especially as the man in this situation, I have had to come to grips with the fact that the fate of somebody's life was literally in my hands. The choices were the same, it had always been to either go against all demands to end things and start a family with her anyway or the grim alternative of simply giving in to cultural differences and family demands and yielding the victory to Tribalism, saying "You won again, have it your way!"

CHAPTER NINE

~δℓℓ~

HOW DO YOU DEAL?

This thing of ours from the very beginning was a taboo, and we knew it. The spoken and unspoken prohibition of our union based solely on the cultural sense that it is repulsive or, maybe, too sacred for ordinary people like Demi and me, had brought us to this stage. I was for her, and she was for me like the sun and the earth. A kind of shared responsibility that only a few can bare to carry.

As an African, a black man, and a Kenyan, I bent my knees and convictions to excite our forefathers who spread this taboo around. And just like every other individual who had walked this path we were on I forgot to care for my own and carried the problems of others—the problem of Makena's fears and the question of their denial. Society had made and enforced the rules.

So how do you deal when you feel like the choice of love has been taken from you? When the one thing you've prayed for and hoped for all your life is now finally, joyfully yours—but all of a sudden, it's taken from you. How do you honestly move on, when you built your entire life around the foundation of a love that was so pure, so true, so resilient, and so promising, but instead turned sour and dark?

At the core of nearly all the great stories known to man is a distressing conflict between good and evil. This struggle provides the framework and baseline for understanding everything else in and around the story. It defines who the real heroes or heroines are, and who the true villains are.

By giving in to her family's demands and ending our quest, despite her consistency and repeated pleas for me to fight just a little harder to make it work, had made me the monster. Unrecognizable by Demi herself, who'd known a different side of me throughout our years together. Unrecognizable to myself standing in the mirror looking at a person who had gone against the most important promise he'd ever made. I had left her paralyzed, unable to fully move on, unable to be truly free, even after many months of separation with absolutely no contact, because she still had our very last conversation playing in a loop in her heart as though she was still in the very midst of it. In short, I had taken something tangible from her and just moved on with my life, like nothing ever happened, and she was left broken to the core. But I was sure she would. I was certain she would find somebody who would be all I couldn't be and at the times when she needed it the most. He would find favor in Mrs. Eniola, and Mr. Adebiyi's eyes, and Demi would love him unconditionally. It wouldn't matter if it came at the expense of our relationship coming to an end because of our cultural differences or my decisions. But it will be fair.

There was hope before. Just a tiny glimmer against the wind. Like the open eyes of a child reaching out its hand, with fingers extended. It's a choice of meanness or kindness in that moment. I saw that dying ashes and brought the winds to a cold howl. How was our thinking so different from my theirs, so foreigner? How was it that I saw the suffering and choose to make it all the worse?

How do you deal, when all along, you have been honest and made sure your love does your partner the utmost good? When you literally spill sweat, tears, and blood, when you fight for your beloved, defend them from their enemies, their afflictions, and their shortcomings? Not only do you fight for them, but you fight with them, feeding off their devotion, their passion, and their energy, off their encouragement. But then, all of a sudden, they drop their arms, they give up, they pull back and leave you in the middle of the battlefield unwarned and unprotected.

The xenophobic hatred and attacks were only part of the story and not the whole. I still had a responsibility to uphold a promise I had made to Demi a long time ago and had worked to make her believe throughout our relationship. She wasn't always sold on the idea that we were going to be okay, but once she believed, her faith was unwavering, and she was all in. I went through great pains to convince her if we got together and stayed together, we would overcome. I assured her with words and actions that no matter how hard things got, and they would, I was going to stick around, and her future was with me, even if it meant losing it all. So, dropping this in the narrative felt like a blatant betrayal, like I had lied all along. But on my end, I had been honest to the fullest and fought with every fiber in me, I had just fought too long and too hard. I gave up, instead of pushing for the second wind that would force us through to the end.

And Demi was one hundred percent right. Any son or daughter, whether living with their parents or not, should be able to make the adult decision on who they want to spend the rest of their lives with. Our parents, friends, and the people around us should be there to offer their opinion and counsel when sought, but not impose their will, such as arranging a marriage for a daughter against her choice with a man she has never met. Or, going behind their son's back to seek out a bride for him and make deals with the female's parents without having consulted with their son. It might be okay to make suggestions and referrals, but it's never acceptable to force anyone into a situation they are otherwise opposed to, especially one as necessary as marriage.

The girl I dreamt of marrying became the girl I couldn't marry or wouldn't ever marry. We hadn't spoken in weeks, and I had no idea what her condition or situation was, especially given the nature of how our last conversation closed. But distance doesn't separate people, silence does—and I was about to break mine to pieces like shattered glass.

CHAPTER TEN

LOVE, I'M GOOD

Here we are. "I will never leave you" had indeed left his beloved, and "I can't imagine my life without you" had been left behind like forgotten bags at the train shelter. One day you realize it's gone, but simply shrug it off and carry on. Our journey had taken an unexpected turn, and many months had elapsed without a word from each other. Whatever silence is. Is there not always the sound of one's heartbeat? In the daytime, there is light and, in the darkness. For if there is the presence of a soul, there is always something.

Twice in eight months, we reached out to each other, but only to wish the other a customary "happy birthday" message, which was only followed by a cordial "thank you" and "I hope you had a great one."

Life had become a long lonely road that I traversed on my own. Demi nor I ever thought we would end up in this place. We had moved slowly, we had moved fast, and then all love and hope were lost.

In these moments, the whole world could have been blown away in a terrible hurricane. And the only reason I knew the ground still stood there is my feet were bare. All else has dissolved like it was never there to begin with, like the universe hadn't even been created. Life and gain. Loss and pain. I longed for the dawn to come and embrace the land. A reminder to a flickering heart that there are others out there. That there is a whole planet of other conscious beings live, love, and laugh. Alas, all I had was a starless sky, even the moon won't shine. Conceivably she lay anxious, shuddering, behind the dark clouds.

"Happy birthday, Yonas. Hope you're having a good day *praying hands emoji*" the text message read.

The time was 10:55 PM when I felt my cell phone vibrating. I was standing in the midst of friends and loved ones, partying, and having a great time celebrating the day. My entire world stopped as shock and surprise ran through my spine. I didn't want to respond immediately, as though I was pressed or desperate, but I also didn't want to stall and waste too much time with a response, as though I were too busy or ignoring her. The timing was a little bit off as well, as I was standing in a lounge filled with loved ones, friends, and family, all gathered to cheer me in celebration of my twenty-seventh year on earth.

"Demi! Thank you. It was blessed for real—another calendar year in the books. I'm grateful," I responded, sending a text back at 10:58 PM with a smile on my face. To the people around me, it may have just appeared to be a look of happiness from the proper time we were having, but to me, it was much more than that, even though I knew the reality was I had let go of the best thing that ever happened in my life.

She knew how much I hated birthdays; I have never been a fan of my birthday. Like the line goes by the late great Biggie Smalls, "Birthdays were the worst days!" and this was exceptionally true for me. Growing up, I never had the privilege or experienced the joy of celebrating the day I was born. It just wasn't that big a deal in my household. I only came to realize how big a deal birthday was to others when I moved to the states and saw how seriously my high school mates took their special day. It did something to me though, it made me sad and incredibly lonely whenever my birthday rolled around, for I never had all the festivities planned, or fresh outfits, or a plethora of people texting me well wishes. It was always a sad day for me, as I couldn't help but compare with my friends who always went all out for their birthdays—going on group trips, organizing grand functions at large venues with hired DJs, doing photoshoots, and receiving gifts. I, on the other hand, usually just got a couple "HBD" text messages.

I hated birthdays, and maybe it was my fault for not making it all that I wanted it to be for myself, but Demi had always made it a point to try to compensate on this special day, and make sure I was filled with joy and happiness. Her efforts never came to life as much as she wanted to because of the great distance that separated us and troubles that always seem to arise last-minute, like her parents barring her from traveling to see me when I would have wanted to enjoy her presence the most. But she always tried.

To hear from her, especially at this timing and on this day, even though we hadn't spoken in a while, was distinct. It was also weird, as our separation was still somewhat fresh, and I knew I couldn't keep the conversation via text messaging going much longer. I wanted to respect her space, because she deserved it after putting up such a hard fight and only getting cruel heartbreak in the end. She deserved her space, and I really had nothing to say or offer at this time that she wanted to hear. I knew she was over me. She had to have been. In fact, those were her parting words as we got off the phone a few months earlier.

"You don't know what you're losing, Yonas," she had said, fighting through tears, pausing between each word to catch her breath as her voice thundered through the cell phone speaker.

"Promise me that if this is really it, then you won't hit me up down the road and try to get back together.

Promise me you will leave me alone," she had demanded, proceeding to emphasize that she had given me her all and tried to build her life around the prospect of us, even if that meant losing her family.

But I had let her down, I had lost her trust. Much more than that, I had lost her altogether, and this time, there wasn't anything I could do to regain her or her trust. At that exact moment, as I stood in the midst of all the fun, music, laughter, and ambiance around me, the folks gathered around having a great time, completely oblivious to my disengagement from the festivities around me…all I could think about was how much I had messed up, and what I had truly lost. I was confronted by the truth. There was no escape from the things I had done, no matter how influenced they may had been by our cultural differences or the demands from our families to separate.

Eighty-nine days between my birthday and Demi's birthday, and I knew that would be my target date to execute this plan. It would take me awhile to plan it right, and so I began. Distance doesn't separate people, silence does, and not having contact with Demi made it even more difficult to fan the dying flame of the love and affection I once had for Demi. But time doesn't heal wounds, contrary to popular belief, it only conceals. The fact of the matter is, true love doesn't die, it only multiplies under the proper circumstances.

I had experienced loneliness like never before. It

was as though her attention was a million miles away and between us was a frozen ocean. I had let go of the one thing that kept me warm. And so, the only way to rekindle this, I thought, was to go back to the start and remind myself of why I pursued the one I loved, why I went through all I had gone through to try and make it work, and why I couldn't let my enemies get the victory over me. Social media was my only window into Demi's life, though to this point I had refrained from visiting her social media page, to protect my own heart and also respect whatever she did with her life. But going back to those same pictures that first attracted me to this dark-skinned, natural-haired, wide smiling, thick, Christ-honoring African beauty was the beginning. But much more than just a few photos I had with me in my possession something tangible, something I needed her to see, and to do that, I needed to see her in person, even though I was certain that wouldn't be an easy task.

They say if you let love go and it comes back to you, it's real, but I wasn't about to sit around and wait for Demi to come back and plead to be in my life. Not with that philosophy. That was the last thing she would do, given what I had done to her, but I knew one thing was for certain—she had a calm spirit and would, at the very least, speak to me. So, I waited and prayed, and when her birthday week rolled around, I reached out to her the day before.

"Birthday tomorrow!" I wrote carefully choosing each word with precision. "I trust you're looking forward to it. Wishing you blessings, have an excellent one."

And as careering a she has always been, she responded within minutes, and we proceeded to have a conversation via text about the concern of every girl or woman who knows her time in the dating pool and to play around is not without limits.

"Had my life planned till this moment, but God had other plans, I guess," she said.

I knew exactly what she meant. All her life, she'd expected to be happily married and living her dreams building a home by twenty-five years old. Even still, she expressed immense thankfulness for life and appreciated me reaching out. I absolutely didn't mind talking to her—this was the perfect opportunity to ask what I had been waiting to ask her for all the months between out birthdays. I just wanted one more chance to see her in Houston. I had a gift for her, something I'd been working on for almost several months. A book.

The book we had joked about writing, to tell our story and inspire others if we ever made it through the horrors and pains of our love story. A book to serve as a reminder that it is all worth it, and there is happiness in the end. Except at this point, our story didn't really have a happy ending. It was a tragedy from the outside looking in, but I knew it hadn't yet been written in full.

My request was simple but bold: "Give me twenty minutes of your time," I asked Demi on the phone while I pleaded for a chance to come up to Houston to meet and talk, even just for a few minutes, only the two of us.

She had no idea what was coming her way, and I had no idea what I was about to get myself into, but all I knew was I had a plan that I absolutely needed to work. I prayed endlessly about it. But one thing was for sure—I was bent on making it right and actually claiming back what I believed was mine, what was taken from me, what I had lost.

This was unlike any previous trip down south, as I could hardly stop thinking of what could go wrong or right. I always enjoyed my time in Houston, especially in the winter months, and this time was no different. Large parts of the city had just had their first real snow of the season, with several inches of snow on the ground, and the sound of cars driving through wet, slushy streets heard from miles away. I was just finishing up a delicious bowl of shrimp and grits in The Lakeview restaurant when I looked up and saw Demi walking in and over to the table I had reserved. The timing could not have been more perfect. It's usually the nerves that make me feel like my stomach is empty, the same feeling I sometimes get before getting on stage to perform for a crowd. All I needed was a quick bite.

It was cold and wet outside, and she had on black

cotton gloves, and a long black peacoat, which she took off immediately after greeting me with a side hug, the kind of hug girls give guys at church, or that you give the colleague you really aren't fond of at their goodbye party. It felt a little unusual at first, but was understandable, given the nature of our relationship at this point and the setting in which we were meeting. I could understand why she wasn't as open and welcoming as in times past. She even left her gloves and scarf on, as though she didn't plan to stay long.

"One black coffee and one chai tea with one cream one sugar," the waitress said, gently placing the cups on the table in front of us.

"Aww, you remembered I love chai tea!" Demi exclaimed with a happy and pleasant smile on her face as she met my eyes.

"Of course!" I responded, "One creamer and one sugar, right?" I thanked her for honoring the invitation and taking the time to meet with me. She didn't have to, and truth be told, I felt undeserving of the warm welcome I had gotten from her thus far.

We sat facing each other at opposite sides of the square table. Along with the two cups of warm beverages, a paperback copy of the complete, unreleased and edited manuscript copy of the book sat on the table. She could hardly take her eyes off it from the moment she sat down, almost in disbelief, as she knew exactly what it was.

"You'll be the first person to read this completed piece of work in its entirety, as promised," I said as I picked it up from the table and handed it over to her.

"Yonas, this is huge! I don't even know how to feel about this now, as a lot has changed since we last talked about you writing this book..." she paused, then continued. "I definitely want to con—"

"Listen, I know it's hitting you differently now that it's actually in front of you," I blurted out, cutting her short before she could finish saying her congratulations.

I had always found it extremely easy to express myself to Demi, no matter what emotions and thoughts I had. But in this very moment, what I was about to say and do could not have been more difficult, as I was almost paralyzed by nervousness and stumbling over my words. Before Demi, I never took a chance at love, because I was scared my heart would break, or I would end up breaking somebody else's heart. In the end, both things happened, and to the one I loved with every fiber in my body. And she was right there. Everything I ever wanted and needed was sitting right in front of me.

It's like time stood still, and yet, I was feeling so much.

"We can be champions, Demi," I professed. "We can own our story and change the narrative."

I had rehearsed and rehearsed this very moment in my head, over and over again for many weeks and all the way through the flight. As I got closer and closer to the reason why I so wanted to meet, I could feel it in my blood, that something about her energy that felt so right every time we touched. It was familiar, and I was still in its presence.

"What are you getting at?" she asked with a puzzled face, as she could tell I was leading up to something unpredictable. It was as though she was curious to know what the punch line was, but at the same time, didn't want me to carry on with it for fear of the predicament it might put her in.

I reached in my coat pocket and pulled out a small black box, opening it to reveal a white gold ring with a round center diamond and a baguette on either side. The exact same ring cut by the exact same jeweler Demi and I had handpicked, pulled from all the years of screenshots, texts, and Social media photos of ring styles she was into and would love. You know, the regular conversation every interested girl loves to have when she wants to make sure her man knows exactly what kind of ring she would die for.

"I want you to marry me, Demi," I said, looking directly in her eyes as I slowly reached across the table to grab her hands.

"Oh, God!" she quietly exclaimed, falling back into her chair in complete shock.

Her eyes were wide, and she seemed to briefly be struck speechless like she was scared to respond. But before she could gather any words to answer me, I continued on. "I want us to do what we should have done a year or two ago!" I said.

"I don't care what happens, in fact I'm more than ready. I'm prepared. I've got the perfect plan! All you have to do is say the word and the rest of our lives will be ours to live!"

But before Demi could say a word, tears started streaming down her face.

"I know it's a lot to handle right now, but I'm here all weekend and for as long as you need me to be!" I pleaded while handing her a napkin to dry off her face.

"You have no idea, Yonas," she responded. Hearing her voice at this moment was simultaneously comforting, as I had been the only one speaking for what felt like an eternity, and also scary, as that wasn't exactly the kind of response I was hoping for at that particular moment.

"...I can't, Yonas," she whispered. "He proposed a couple of months ago, and I said yes," she continued, as she removed the black glove from her left hand, revealing a diamond ring cut so similar to the one she'd always wanted, just like the one that sat in the box right in front of her on the table.

"I'm sorry!" she said. "I really just wanted to honor the promise we made a long time ago about this meeting. Maybe I was just seeking closure." she continued.

Her response was so unexpected, so far from what I wanted from her, I just stared at her open-mouthed. My brain froze, formulating no thoughts except to index that I was in utter shock. It splintered inside me, causing more pain than a migraine. I slowly closed my mouth, then looked at my toes before peeking back up to catch her eye.

Still processing the weightiness and shock of the moment, I couldn't coordinate the right words in my brain to articulate a response. Still, I listened.

"I couldn't tell you over the phone either, and wanted to also take this opportunity to break the news to you."

The scene was quite unbelievable, but just as real as the heart attack, I felt like I was about to have, shockingly real. My mind was sent whirling, unable to process or register the images my eyes transmitted to it. I looked away, then looked back. I looked away once again, then looked back to see if it was still there. And it was. I wasn't trained to deal with this kind of emergency.

It indeed was the end of all ends for us, as this was confirmation that she was not only through and moved on from our love saga, but done with the meeting. She gently put her glove back on and reached for her coat as she continued her apology.

"I'm so sorry, Yonas, but I just can't...everything we had and shared is in the past now." She concluded.

All I could do was watch, speechless, as she stood up to leave.

"I understand if we never speak or see each other again," she said.

I boiled up in anger and resentment at myself, at Makena at Mrs. Eniola, at Demi, but no matter how much I searched, I couldn't find a justifiable reason as to why they were to blame. Or even the Tribal differences that separated us. I let this happen, and I had nothing to say at that particular moment, as I watched the woman, I always thought I was born to be with walk out of my life for good. And then it hit me; I let her go, I let us go. In holding on to the fear of the unknown, fear of archaic and baseless traditions, fear of the power of love, and fear of victory through hardships, I let go of the one thing and the one person who was the key to unlocking all those questions I needed answers to and could only experience with and through her.

*****

At this point, I could see my good friend Tayo, who had been so graciously and attentively listening in silence, was drowning in desolation for me. His eyes shifted from side to side as they became glazed with tears. They dripped from his eyelids with each blink, sliding down his cheeks. My heart sank in my chest as I reflected back on my story. I could not help but join in with him as we both let our tears flow. For him, it was a reminder of the hurt and pain he had fought through before marrying his bride. They lived in marital bliss and were building a warm and beautiful home, but it came at the expense of emotional and psychological torture to the both of them, much like Demi and I had gone through.

This is why he understood me and why I ran to him for comfort and to vent my emotions.

"I just wish it could have ended differently for you guys, Yonas," Tayo said to me, fighting back the tears and drying the streaks on his face.

"I know," I responded. "Like it's really over, but not over, you know what I mean?"

It was my tears that kept my soul-driven in this furnace of pain and agony. Was our ending really supposed to be a happy one? Only the good LORD knows. We dreamt and spoke about it with great anticipation, despite everything. With each day that passed was another blow on the nail that sealed the coffin. I could not extinguish what had been but only carry myself forward until it came a time when this searing pain was distant enough for me to forget it more than I could remember. And that meant forgetting about Demi, too. If she were to be the happy bride, I had always wanted her to be, and she had said yes to this guy, then I had to keep a reasonable distance and let it be.

For my family, it was a sigh of relief to learn I was

no longer with Demi and that she was engaged to be married very soon. I was always reminded of "the bullet I had dodged" if I, in their words, had "stubbornly" went into that family against their counsel. To them, separating from Demi was the biggest and best decision I had ever made, and I would do well to stay away from that family and situation forever.

"You're very young and have the rest of your life to find somebody who will love you and whose family will accept you," they would say. Week after week, and day after day, they peeled the flesh off my wounds with their words.

But was this wise? Was there truth to what they were saying and what I thought? Was I just going to accept defeat again, and let things play out as they stood? Or was it not truly over until the pastor says those famous words? As far as I was concerned, this was only the halfway point, and I had to go all the way, even if it meant breaking down some doors to do so. Sitting across from Demi in a restaurant was like a soft knock on her heart. If the outcome was to be different, then I had to come hard—I had to take it all the way.

AFTERWORD

Polarization between two cultures brings out the dark side of Tribalism. In saying there is a negative infers, there is real and actual greatness to Tribalism. What you just witnessed is the brutal and harsh effect of the negative aspect of the subject on demand. But first, we have to define what Tribalism is.

A tribe is a group of people that are connected in a meaningful way based on something they share in common that is of significance to them. For most of the world, when the conversation of Tribalism is on the table, it is generally centered around politics. For example, political Tribalism will be Republican party core beliefs and democratic party core beliefs in the United States system of government. In the African context or for our purpose here, it shows in the food we eat, the lifestyle we live, the fabric we wear, or the language we speak.

This construction could also be based on religion,

ethnicity, ideologies, nationality, class, and kinship. What matters is the connection binding individuals together into a group or Tribe allows them to make the distinction between "us" who are the members of the said group vs. "them" who are the people outside the group.

Fundamentally, Tribalism is those patterns of behaviors and attitudes we tend to adopt when we come to identify with our Tribe. In other words, we could use the "we" and "them" adjectives defined by tribal boundaries to make distinctions on what we deem to be normative judgments. Our food is better, and their food is not. We are good, they are bad. They are wrong; we are right. Our beliefs and ways are true, and their beliefs and ways are wayward. These judgments support behaviors, what we say, how we communicate it and group our moral physiology or composition.

Philosophers of old in centuries past call this type of reasoning or means by which we make judgments epistemology. A term mostly only used in Sunday school or maybe seminary. A word that mostly could be defined as the study of the origins and nature of knowledge. Judgment about what constitutes knowledge. For instance, when we claim that our moral physiology is "group-ish", it is also to infer that our epistemic physiology is group-ish or tribal.

They are connected. But functional physiology

will demand we keep the two separate and distinct from each other. However, in the course of understanding human behavior and trying to figure out how human beings actually form judgments and make decisions, we will find that we cannot separate our moral physiology from our epistemic physiology. They both develop from the same cognitive system, thus making our tribal physiology both a moral and epistemic physiology. That is, Tribalism defined.

Tribalism per se, in and of itself, is not dangerous. But the dangers of Tribalism are driven by polarization, the measure of the magnitude of differences between two different tribal groups. The ratio of how large or small those differences are and the impact they make on our judgments. Where polarization increases, common ground decreases, making it harder and all the tougher to identify areas of agreement that we could apply for arbitrating in opinions. We focus more on our differences as a reflection of our incompatible worldviews than our areas of agreeance, and we hit a point where we feel an urge to separate. Peaceful coexistence between us seems impossible and our instinct to adapt by segregating kicks in.

This does sometimes lead to a worse kind of behavior in our relations to one another—for example, prejudice--the discrimination within one's own race, violence, atrocity, genocide. Even when we don't get to the point of violence, we are left with situations where our "in groups" are dominated by hostility, and fear. The point where we cut ourselves from other points of view and only look to our Tribe for guidance on what to believe and who to trust. Everyone outside this bubble becomes liar, untrustworthy, and unreliable. On the flip side we experience a sense of belonging, of comradery, and a healthy community.

When your parents, the ones who raised you and whose respect and love you treasure disapprove of your partner, it hurts. Though for many of us we obey and act accordingly.

Like a black man in his twenties is struggling or caught between his mother and his wife. The man, a Chinese with a mother who expects her son's wife to obey her and wait for her when she visits just as she did for her mother-in-law in her back in her own time. The man, whose American wife works with all diligence and integrity to appease her husband's mother who can't help in starting dinner or strike a conversation when she visits. Who complains always, stresses the daughter-in-law to tears and sleepless nights.

Like a young Latina female with a white boyfriend whose father goes on and one about illegal immigration in the United States whenever she visits. Nobody can shut him up, she fakes a smile through it every time, but it results into a fight with her boyfriend later on because she thinks he should be able to stop his father or stand up for her and their relationship.

Like a Rwandese girl with a Rwandese boyfriend who wishes to marry her but they're both from different ethnic groups and they know their parents will never agree or bless the union. They've been secretly seeing each other for 4 years.

Like the people in these three different real-life examples, there are millions of others in love. They want their family to respect and love the person they've chosen to do life with. But instead, the family sometimes doesn't always see past misplaced prejudices, traditions, and values. Your boyfriend or girlfriend could be the sweetheart and the amazing person they are, but your family would be blind to it, only seeing something wrong with your person and the culture they come from. Bridging this divide that has crippled relationships and marriages for centuries can only be fought with clear intentions, commitment, and the compromises both parties are willing to make to stay together. The constant rejection and disapproval often manifest itself by intense but unexpressed anger seething under the surface of bashful words and despicable actions.

This undermines your relationship and puts the couple in a dreadful bond. Heeded and responding to either side, your family or partner makes the other feel disrespected or abandoned. As the partner, you will always feel the pressure of having to prove yourself to be worthy because you are the focus of dislike. These efforts can quickly turn into resentment and anger towards the love of your life that spills into a tragic breakup of a beautiful relationship.

The pendulum swings from less dramatic situation to even deadly ones where lives have been lost. So do the solutions and fortunately there are the solutions that don't result to the death scene in Romeo and Juliet. Like Tevye in Fiddler or Robert in Downton, there are families who eventually accept their adult children's choices and even give their full sincere blessings. It takes patience, hard work and willingness, however, and doesn't happen by magic or by argument. There are those whose battle has more twists, turns, and detours. Demi and Yonas were part of the unfortunate bunch.

A careful study of the text will show a member of any tribe could marry any other nation and Tribe; as tribal identity has always been passed down through the lineage of the father. For example, if Jane, an Asher-ite, marries John, a Levite, their children will be Levites. You would probably still identify Jane herself as being from the Tribe of Asher, but it would not change much. E.g. we know that Samson's father was from Dan, but his mother from Judah. There are of course, as some would argue, vast cultural differences to consider that would make marriages more difficult. Interestingly enough, many of these cultural differences in present times or Biblically were not based on race but on the Tribe that one belonged to. When the Israelites left Egypt they were joined by a "mixed multitude" of Gentiles from every nation and skin color on the earth, and once they passed through and were baptized in the Red Sea, and given God's Law, they were also considered to be Israelites, and were expected to keep the same Law as the Native Born (Numbers 15, Isaiah 56, Psalm 119, Matthew 5:17-19, Revelations 1). We also find Moses the Levite marrying an Ethiopian woman and those who spoke against them had their hand turn leprous. Boaz of Judah married a Moabitess, and Rahab the Canaanite was married to one of the Israelite spies. This was possible because they were physically grafted into the Tribe of Judah (regardless of race) just as all believers are spiritually grafted in. Inheritance was not an issue, and they adopted the culture of the Tribe of their husband's and abandoned their lives and customs they kept as unbelievers.

When the good Samaritan, our LORD Jesus told in a parable to an expert of the Law, helped a Levite Jew out a ditch, he broke a tribal code. A very radical act at his time. In our time, though we boast in and celebrate diversity in our relationships, our enlightened ideologies oftentimes run against to our deep-seated tribal conservatism. We need not pretend to care when in all reality, we don't. We need not throw ourselves into furies of false benevolence. It only sets us from the intimacy of reasonable care and creates false emotions and collective panic. If we are honest with ourselves as the enlightened ones of this generation, a good look at our souls will reveal that we are not as gracious and loving to the stranger as we should or would like to be.

There is beauty in learning a new culture, a woman leaving her father's house and cleaving to her husband's and growing with his culture while still maintaining the beauty of the values her mother and folks raised her with. The world is one big melting pot of cultures, and if any man and woman find love in each other and desire to pursue the covenant of marriage together, there shouldn't be any man or woman who stops this union based only on the fact that they are not from the same country or Tribe.

What we love, if we are honest, is our Tribe, our country, our family, and our small intimate communities. Not Africa or whatever the case may be.

Nothing brings Africans, in the continent or the diaspora, together in unity more than football or the sport the white man calls soccer does. So, to put it in terms of a sport that we shared a common love for to bring a reality to light for you my beloved friend, it brings us together like a various spice melting in a pot to create a sweet flavor of jollof rice. It wets our passions, leaves us screaming at the top of our voices shouting "GOOOOOOAAAAL!" in a triumphant celebration, pledging to our nation, and sets our hearts ablaze racing like we won a hundred-meter dash. A win unites the nation and brings the community closer in unity, holding the honor as one Nigeria, one Cameroon, or Ghana or Ethiopia or even America.

In the same token, nothing divides and separates us more than football or the sport the white man calls soccer. The game is competitive; it tears us apart like war tears up a family. It ignites anger, fuels our hatred for defending "our people," and separating ourselves from "those people." The miss of a goal becomes a chance to tear down our neighbors with our tongues, fashioned like a weapon and our tribes the armor. We manifest into a nation full of excellent pretenders oblivious to what unites us as we are trapped in bubbles of ethnicity because one of us has betrayed us by missing a goal or a penalty kick. That is Tribalism.

The way I see it we have two major problems; on the one hand, we are dealing with an identity crisis and on the other hand a case of psychological homelessness. So, the question remains, when are we one people? Think of your birthplace and ask yourself, when are we one nation? A greater Africa in the continent and especially in the diaspora, requires that we break out of our ethnic molds. The identities we assume are a choice that determines who we cast away or who embrace. No football or sports team wins by attacking itself but until we hate the Tribalism, racism and xenophobia that separates us more than we hate each other we remain as anti-African as the oppressors that oppress us, and love will never reign in our generations to come.

It becomes a lot more complicated with two people of different religions like Christian and Muslim for example, who practice and take their faith serious to be yoked together in matrimony. Even I would strongly advise those parties to think twice and hard about entering into such a union. As I stated in the preface, one of the reason why I wrote this book was that not only is my story my power but because Demi and Yonas were not the only people who have had to go through such a painful and difficult situation and neither would we be the last. If you find yourself in this story, be encouraged. Whatever the outcome is the future is always brighter.

I heard somebody say it is a blessing to belong, but Tribalism is the burden. We have a critical choice to make as a society: are we going to live in harmony, with respect, acceptance, and love, or are we going to live in perpetual animosity, ostracization, and alienation.

Our future depends on the decision.

ℐℓℓ

'No Such Thing As Halfway', gives voice to both young men and young ladies as they tell the story of their long-distance romance and the forces that threaten to tear it apart. Demi and Yonas have been dating for almost six years since they met on social media. Though their families expect them to only take spouses from their respective tribes and/or country, Demi and Yonas promise each other to fight the traditions and break the mold. Eight years into their long-distance romance, after wearying and extensive battles with both Demi's family and Yonas family, their future is endangered when Yonas bails out of their pact, cascading their relationship into demise. Depleted, contrite, and filled with regret, Yonas knows the only way to save their relationship and keep his promise to Demi is to go back for his beloved. But is he too late?

An exhilarating novel of immeasurable emotional power, No Such Thing As Halfway asks how much we are willing to sacrifice for the sake of love or for the sake of the family.

ABOUT THE AUTHOR

Achu 'RifleX' Ebong Mba is a musical artist, host of the acclaimed Stuck in The Middle podcast, and author of *No Such Thing As Halfway: A Novel*. With over a decade studying and writing literature for published blogs, RifleX has a uniquely powerful voice that shines through in his book on love, tribalism, and the importance we place on family traditions. He has a Bachelor of Arts in Communications and Master of Science in Cyber Security degree from the University of Maryland and is a proud member of the Sigma Tau Delta International English Honor Society. RifleX lives and works mostly out of his home in Laurel, Maryland and dreams of a time when he can spend his summers in Cameroon.

Connect with the Author
info@iamriflex.com

WWW.IAMRIFLEX.COM